Highways to Prosperity

The Economic Case for Road Infrastructure Development in Zambia

Mabvuto Kaela

CONTENTS

Reflection and Action Plan:

Preface

In the creation of 'Highways to Prosperity: The Economic Case for Road Infrastructure Development in Zambia', we have leveraged the power of Artificial Intelligence (AI) tools. These advanced technologies have been instrumental in helping us gather and analyze data, generate insights, and craft a comprehensive narrative for this book.

The use of AI in this process underscores the transformative potential of these technologies. By automating complex tasks and processing vast amounts of information, AI and Machine Learning (ML) can democratize knowledge, making it more accessible and empowering individuals with great ideas who may not have had the means to pursue them otherwise.

In this book, we explore not only the role of road infrastructure in driving economic growth and development but also the potential of AI and ML technologies to revolutionize Zambia's road network and transportation systems. As we get into these topics, we hope to inspire a conversation about the importance of embracing these technologies in our quest for economic prosperity. This is the moon-shot moment for Zambia.

Just as we have used AI to bring this book to life, we believe that Zambia can harness the power of AI and ML to pave its own highway to prosperity. By integrating these technologies into its strategic planning, Zambia can enhance the efficiency and effectiveness of its infrastructure management, optimize logistics and supply chains, and make data-driven decisions that boost economic growth.

In the end, this book is not just about roads or technology. It's about the power of ideas and the potential of innovation to transform our world. We hope that it will inspire you to think differently about the challenges we face and the solutions we can create.

Together, let's hit the road to a brighter, more prosperous future.

INTRODUCTION

Welcome to "Highways to Prosperity: The Economic Case for Road Infrastructure Development in Zambia." This book is an in-depth exploration of the transformative potential of road infrastructure in shaping Zambia's economic landscape, fostering regional integration, and the revolutionary role that Artificial Intelligence (AI) and Machine Learning (ML) can play in redefining Zambia's transportation systems and road networks.

This book is a journey that bridges my personal experiences with extensive research, reflections, and innovative ideas on this topic. It weaves together economic theory, data analysis, real-world examples, and the transformative power of AI tools to make a compelling case for prioritizing road infrastructure development in Zambia.

Imagine the joy of a child visiting their grandmother's village for the first time, not hindered by the distance or the state of the roads. Picture the thrill of a family exploring the beauty of our national parks, no longer reserved for tourists due to prohibitive prices and inadequate roads. Envision the growth of local businesses, no longer stifled by the lack of access to markets. This is the Zambia we aspire to create, and it starts with developing our road infrastructure.

The book begins by exploring the economics of roads, discussing how they facilitate trade, stimulate economic growth, and impact various sectors of the economy. We then venture into the current state of Zambia's road network, examining its strengths and areas for improvement. The subsequent chapters discuss the impact of road infrastructure on GDP, the role of road infrastructure in regional integration, and the various financing options for road infrastructure.

Recognizing that resources are limited, we also discuss how to balance infrastructure development with other national priorities. We then draw lessons from case studies of successful road infrastructure projects in other countries. In the final chapters, we explore the potential role of AI and ML in transforming Zambia's road network and how these technologies can be harnessed to optimize infrastructure management and logistics.

This book is intended for a broad audience, including policymakers, economists, students, and anyone interested in Zambia's development. It aims to spark a national conversation about the importance of road infrastructure and provide a roadmap for making it a national priority. Each chapter of this book concludes with reflection points and action plans, designed to engage you, the reader, and encourage you to think more deeply about the topics discussed.

Whether you're a seasoned economist or a curious layperson, I hope this book provides you with valuable insights and provokes thoughtful discussion about the future of Zambia's road network. Let's embark on this journey together toward understanding the highways to prosperity.

1

THE ECONOMICS OF ROADS

"Infrastructure is much more important than architecture." - Rem Koolhaas.

As we embark on this enlightening journey into the world of road economics, we will unravel the intricate tapestry that weaves together the fundamental principles underpinning this field. Roads, in their simplest form, are more than just physical conduits for movement and exchange. They are the arteries of our economies, facilitating the lifeblood of goods, services, and people, fostering trade, enhancing connectivity, and promoting socio-economic integration. Yet, their influence extends far beyond these tangible benefits.

Roads are catalysts for economic metamorphosis. They stimulate investment, enhance productivity, and create jobs, driving economic growth and prosperity. They open up remote and underdeveloped areas to new opportunities, paving the way for their integration into the broader economy. Moreover, by improving access to markets and services, roads can play a significant role in reducing poverty and promoting inclusive growth.

In the context of Zambia, a landlocked country nestled in the heart of Southern Africa, the importance of road infrastructure is amplified. Given its geographical location, Zambia relies heavily on its road network for both domestic and international trade. Therefore, investing in road infrastructure can have a significant impact on Zambia's economic development.

As we go deeper into this chapter, we will also explore the transformative potential of Artificial Intelligence (AI) and Machine Learning (ML) technologies. These technologies, which we will review in greater detail in the final chapter, can revolutionize Zambia's road network and transportation systems, optimizing infrastructure management, logistics, and supply chains, thereby enhancing the efficiency and effectiveness of Zambia's road network.

This chapter sets the stage for the rest of the book, where we will look into the current state of Zambia's road network, the impact of road infrastructure on GDP, the role of road infrastructure in regional integration, the security of the roads, and the various financing options for road infrastructure. We will also discuss how to balance infrastructure development with other national priorities and draw lessons from case studies of successful road infrastructure projects in other countries.

So, let's embark on this journey together, as we explore the highways to prosperity for Zambia. Let's grasp this moment as the "moon-shot" moment it can be and unravel the economics of roads to discover how they can pave the way to a brighter, more prosperous future for Zambia.

1.1 Understanding Road Economics

Road economics, a specialized niche within the broader discipline of economics, looks into the intricate dynamics of production, distribution, and consumption of goods and services tied to road infrastructure. This field transcends the physical construction of roads, extending into the complex network of activities and decisions that envelop these infrastructures.

An arial depiction of Road Economics

At its core, road economics grapples with the concept of resource allocation. It scrutinizes how resources—such as labor, materials, and capital—are allocated and utilized for the construction, maintenance, and operation of roads. These decisions are far from trivial. They involve meticulous consideration of various factors, including geographical terrain, population density, traffic volume, and the potential economic return of a road project.

Consider the construction of a road, for instance. This is a significant economic activity in itself. It involves the mobilization of a wide range of resources, from the raw materials used in the construction to the labor force employed in the project. The process stimulates economic activity, creates jobs, and can lead to the development of related industries, such as construction materials and equipment. For example, in 2019, the construction industry in Zambia employed approximately 4.5% of the total workforce, a figure that underscores the sector's significance in job creation.

Maintenance and operation, on the other hand, are ongoing activities that ensure the functionality and safety of roads. These activities require regular expenditure, providing a steady stream of jobs and contributing to the economy on a continual basis. In Zambia, for instance, the Road Development Agency (RDA) spent approximately ZMW 2.5 billion on road maintenance and rehabilitation in 2020, highlighting the economic activity generated by these operations.

However, road economics extends beyond these direct impacts. It also studies the indirect effects of road infrastructure on the economy. For instance, a well-developed road network can enhance connectivity, reduce transportation costs, and facilitate trade, thereby fostering economic growth. It can also attract investment, stimulate tourism, and open up remote areas to economic activities. In Zambia, the tourism sector, which heavily relies on good road infrastructure, contributed approximately 7.2% to the country's GDP in 2018.

Moreover, road economics also involves the study of the economic costs associated with roads. These include not only the direct costs of construction, maintenance, and operation but also the indirect costs, such as traffic congestion, air pollution, and road accidents. In 2019, Zambia recorded approximately 32,392 road traffic accidents, a figure that under-scores the economic and social costs associated with road safety.

In essence, road economics provides a framework for understanding the economic implications of roads. It helps policymakers make informed decisions about road infrastructure development, ensuring that resources are used efficiently and that the benefits of roads are maximized while their costs are minimized. By delving into road economics, we can gain valuable insights into how roads can contribute to economic development and prosperity. This understanding is crucial as we envision a future where Zambia's road network is a key driver of its economic growth and prosperity.

1.2 The Role of Roads in Economic Development

Roads, often metaphorically referred to as the arteries of a nation's economy, serve as the vital lifelines that interconnect people, goods, and services. They are the tangible embodiment of connectivity, enabling the seamless flow of trade and commerce. A well-developed road network can act as a potent catalyst for a country's economic productivity, influencing it in several significant ways:

Bolstering Trade

Roads are the fundamental channels that enable the efficient movement of goods from production sites to markets. They form the backbone of domestic and international trade, allowing businesses to reach customers across vast distances. But their role extends beyond mere transportation. Roads also enable regions to specialize in what they do best, whether it's agriculture, manufacturing, or services. By reducing the cost of transporting goods, roads enable regions to focus on producing what they're most efficient at, leading to increased productivity and economic output. This concept, known as comparative advantage in economics, is a key driver of trade and economic growth. For instance, in Zambia, the agricultural sector, which heavily relies on road infrastructure for transporting produce, contributed approximately 6.7% to the country's GDP in 2018.

Connecting People

Roads are not just about goods; they're also about people. They connect people to jobs, education, healthcare, and other essential services. This connectivity can have profound implications for living standards and economic opportunities. For instance, by improving access to education and healthcare, roads can enhance human capital, a critical ingredient for economic development. They can also reduce the cost and time of commuting, increasing labor mobility and productivity. Furthermore, roads can facilitate social interactions and cultural exchanges, contributing to social cohesion and national unity. In Zambia, for example, the construction of the Kazungula Bridge has significantly reduced travel time and costs for people living in the border regions, enhancing their access to essential services and economic opportunities.

Attracting Investment

A robust and efficient road network can be a magnet for investment. By reducing the cost and risk associated with transporting goods and services, roads can make a region more attractive to investors. This can lead to the establishment of new businesses, the expansion of existing ones, and the creation of jobs, all of which contribute to economic growth. Moreover, by improving access to markets, roads can enhance the profitability of investments, encouraging further capital inflow. For instance, the Lusaka South Multi-Facility Economic Zone (LS-MFEZ), which boasts excellent road connectivity, has attracted over USD 1 billion in investment since its establishment.

In essence, roads are much more than physical infrastructures; they are enablers of economic development. They facilitate trade, connect people, and attract investment, driving economic growth and prosperity. However, the benefits of roads are not automatic; they depend on the quality of the road network and the context in which it operates. In the following sections, we will get into these aspects, exploring how road infrastructure can be leveraged for economic development in the Zambian context.

1.3 Unleashing the Social Potential of Roads

Beyond their economic impact, roads also hold significant social value. They serve as vital lifelines, connecting people to essential services, fostering social inclusion, and playing a crucial role in poverty reduction, particularly in rural areas. However, the social benefits of roads are not always evenly distributed, and careful planning is needed to ensure that road development benefits all members of society.

Bridging the Gap to Essential Services

Roads are the primary means of access to essential services such as education, healthcare, and social services. In rural areas, where these services are often sparse and dispersed, a well-developed road network can significantly reduce travel times and costs, making these services more accessible. This can lead to improved health outcomes, higher school attendance rates, and greater utilization of social services. For instance, in Zambia, the construction of the Chingola-Solwezi road has significantly improved access to healthcare services for communities living along this corridor.

Fostering Social Inclusion

By connecting remote and marginalized communities to urban centers and markets, roads can promote social inclusion. They can provide rural populations with better access to job opportunities, enable them to sell their products in larger markets, and facilitate their participation in social and cultural activities. This can help to reduce rural-urban disparities, foster social cohesion, and enhance the quality of life for these communities. A case in point is the Mpika-Chinsali road in Zambia, which has opened up previously isolated communities to new economic and social opportunities.

Driving Poverty Reduction

Roads can also play a crucial role in poverty reduction. By reducing transportation costs and improving access to markets and services, they can increase incomes and reduce living costs for poor households. This is particularly important in rural areas, where poverty rates are often higher and access to economic opportunities is more limited. For example, the rehabilitation of the Great East Road in Zambia has led to increased agricultural productivity and incomes for smallholder farmers in the Eastern Province.

A shot above rural Lusaka

Ensuring Equitable Benefits

However, the social benefits of roads are not always evenly distributed. Without careful planning, road development can bypass marginalized communities, exacerbate social inequalities, and lead to negative environmental impacts. Therefore, it's crucial to adopt a people-centered approach to road development, one that considers the needs and perspectives of all members of society, including marginalized and vulnerable groups.

In the context of Zambia, where rural-urban disparities are significant, and many rural communities are isolated, the social value of roads is particularly high. By investing in its road network, Zambia can enhance social inclusion, improve access to services, and contribute to poverty reduction. However, to ensure that these benefits are widely shared, it's crucial to incorporate social considerations into infrastructure planning and decision-making processes. In the following sections, we will explore these issues in more detail, examining how Zambia can leverage its road infrastructure for social development.

1.4 The Economics of Road Infrastructure Investment

Investing in road infrastructure can yield significant economic returns, acting as a catalyst for economic growth and development. However, to make informed decisions about these investments, it's crucial to consider the full range of costs and benefits. This includes not only the direct costs of construction and maintenance but also the indirect costs and benefits, such as the impact on economic activity, the environment, and social equity.

Direct Costs: The Immediate Price Tag

The direct costs of road infrastructure investment include the costs of land acquisition, design and planning, construction, and ongoing maintenance and repair. These costs can be substantial, particularly for large-scale infrastructure projects. For instance, the construction of the Lusaka-Ndola dual carriageway, one of Zambia's most ambitious road projects, is estimated to cost around $1.2 billion. These costs require upfront funding, which can be a challenge for countries with limited fiscal resources. However, these costs can be offset by the economic benefits that road infrastructure can generate, such as increased economic activity and improved access to markets and services.

Indirect Costs: The Hidden Expenses

In addition to these direct costs, road infrastructure investment can also have indirect costs. These can include environmental costs, such as the impact on air quality, noise levels, and natural habitats. There can also be social costs, such as displacement of communities, disruption of local economies, and increased traffic and congestion. These costs are often overlooked in infrastructure planning, but they can be significant and should be factored into investment decisions.

Economic Benefits: The Ripple Effects

On the benefit side, road infrastructure investment can stimulate economic activity, both directly and indirectly. *Directly*, it can generate jobs and income through construction and maintenance activities. For example, the construction of the Kazungula Bridge, linking Zambia and Botswana, created over 500 jobs. *Indirectly*, it can boost economic productivity by reducing transportation costs, improving access to markets, and facilitating trade and commerce. These benefits can lead to increased GDP, higher tax revenues, and improved economic resilience.

Social and Environmental Benefits: The Long-Term Gains

Road infrastructure can also have significant social and environmental benefits. It can improve access to essential services, promote social inclusion, and contribute to poverty reduction. Environmentally, well-planned road projects can help to manage traffic flow, reduce emissions through more efficient vehicle movement, and even contribute to landscape preservation if integrated with green infrastructure strategies.

In conclusion, the economics of road infrastructure investment involves a complex interplay of costs and benefits, both direct and indirect. To make informed investment decisions, it's important to consider all these factors and to adopt a holistic approach to infrastructure planning. This approach should consider not just the financial aspects of infrastructure investment, but also its economic, social, and environmental impacts. In the following sections, we will look more into these issues, exploring the economic case for road infrastructure development in Zambia.

1.5 Embracing the Future: The Transformative Potential of AI and ML in Road Infrastructure

As we cast our gaze towards the horizon of road infrastructure, it's impossible to overlook the transformative potential of Artificial Intelligence (AI) and Machine Learning (ML) technologies. These advanced technologies, which are already reshaping industries worldwide, have the capacity to revolutionize Zambia's road network and transportation systems, offering innovative solutions that could significantly enhance efficiency and effectiveness.

AI and ML are not just buzzwords; they are powerful tools that can analyze vast amounts of data, identify patterns, and make predictions, providing valuable insights for infrastructure management. For instance, these technologies could be used to optimize traffic flow, reducing congestion and improving commute times. They could predict maintenance needs, allowing for proactive repairs that could extend the lifespan of roads and save costs in the long run. They could also improve road safety, analyzing traffic patterns and accident data to identify high-risk areas and suggest interventions.

Moreover, AI and ML can also optimize logistics and supply chains, which are crucial for the efficient movement of goods across the country. Imagine a Zambia where trucks are optimally loaded and routed based on real-time traffic and weather data, reducing delivery times and fuel consumption. This is not a distant dream, but a tangible possibility with AI and ML.

In the final chapter of this book, we will explore more into how Zambia can harness the power of AI and ML to transform its road infrastructure. We will explore real-world examples, discuss potential challenges, and outline a roadmap for integrating these technologies into Zambia's infrastructure strategy. But for now, as we continue to explore the current state and future potential of Zambia's road network, it's important to keep in mind the role these technologies could play in shaping the future of Zambia's transportation systems.

The future of road infrastructure is not just about asphalt and concrete; it's also about data and algorithms. By embracing AI and ML, Zambia can position itself at the forefront of this technological revolution, paving the way for a more connected, efficient, and prosperous future.

1.6 Paving the Way for Progress: The Role of Roads in Regional Development

Roads, often seen as the veins and arteries of a region, play a pivotal role in regional development. They serve as the physical links that connect different regions, facilitate trade, and can help to balance regional disparities in economic development. This role of roads in regional development can be seen in initiatives such as the Belt and Road Initiative (BRI), but it's also evident in the everyday lives of people in regions across the globe.

Connecting Regions: The Lifelines of Local Economies

Roads connect cities, towns, and villages within a region, enabling the movement of people and goods. This connectivity can stimulate economic activity, foster social interaction, and enhance access to services. In rural areas, roads can open up access to markets, jobs, and services, contributing to rural development and poverty reduction. They can transform remote villages into bustling hubs of economic activity, bringing new opportunities and prosperity. In urban areas, roads facilitate commuting, commerce, and urban development, supporting the growth of vibrant, dynamic cities.

Facilitating Trade: The Highways of Commerce

By reducing transportation costs and travel times, roads can facilitate trade within and between regions. They enable businesses to reach larger markets, source inputs more efficiently, and achieve economies of scale. This can boost business competitiveness, stimulate investment, and create jobs. For consumers, improved road connectivity can lead to a wider variety of goods and services, lower prices, and improved living standards. Roads, in essence, are the highways of commerce, driving economic growth and prosperity.

Balancing Regional Disparities: The Bridges to Equality

Roads can also play a role in balancing regional disparities in economic development. By improving connectivity, they can help to spread the benefits of economic growth more evenly across a region. This can help to reduce regional inequalities, foster social cohesion, and promote more balanced and inclusive growth. Roads, in this sense, are the bridges to equality, helping to ensure that all regions can share in the benefits of economic development.

The Belt and Road Initiative (BRI): A Global Example

The BRI, launched by China, is a prime example of how roads and other infrastructure can drive regional development. The initiative aims to improve connectivity across Asia, Africa, and Europe through investments in roads, railways, ports, and other infrastructure. This is expected to facilitate trade, stimulate economic growth, and promote regional integration. The BRI also aims to export China's industrial standards and resolve issues from excess industrial capacity, thereby promoting industrial upgrading and sustainable development in participating countries.

In the context of Zambia, with its strategic location in Southern Africa, roads can play a crucial role in regional development. By improving its road network, Zambia can enhance its connectivity with neighboring countries, facilitate regional trade, and contribute to balanced and inclusive regional development. In the following sections, we will explore these issues in more detail, examining the potential benefits and challenges of road infrastructure development in Zambia. Let's journey together on these roads of regional development, exploring their potential to drive progress and prosperity.

1.7 Navigating the Path: Challenges and Opportunities in Road Infrastructure Development

Road infrastructure development, while holding significant potential benefits, also presents a unique set of challenges that need to be carefully navigated. These include high up-front costs, the need for ongoing maintenance, potential negative environmental and social impacts, and risks associated with infrastructure investments. However, these challenges also present opportunities for countries like Zambia to maximize the economic and social benefits while minimizing the risks and negative impacts.

High Upfront Costs: The Initial Hurdle

Road infrastructure projects often require substantial upfront investment. These costs can pose a significant burden for countries with limited fiscal resources. However, these initial costs can be offset by the long-term economic benefits that road infrastructure can generate, such as increased economic activity, improved access to markets, and enhanced social inclusion. The initial investment, while daunting, can be seen as a seed planted for future economic growth and prosperity.

Ongoing Maintenance: The Lifeline of Roads

Roads require ongoing maintenance to keep them in good condition and to maximize their lifespan. The cost of maintenance can be significant and is often overlooked in infrastructure planning. However, regular maintenance can prevent more costly repairs in the future and can ensure that roads continue to deliver their intended benefits. It's the lifeline that keeps the roads alive and functioning optimally.

Environmental and Social Impacts: The Balancing Act

Road infrastructure development can have negative environmental and social impacts, such as displacement of communities, destruction of natural habitats, and increased air and noise pollution. However, with careful planning and management, these impacts can be minimized. Environmental impact assessments can be used to identify potential impacts and mitigation measures, and community consultation can ensure that the needs and concerns of affected communities are taken into account. It's a delicate balancing act, ensuring development while preserving the environment and social fabric.

Investment Risks: The Calculated Gamble

Infrastructure investments also carry risks, such as delayed returns on investment and the need for debt renegotiation. This has been the case with some Belt and Road Initiative (BRI) projects. However, these risks can be managed through careful project appraisal, prudent fiscal management, and transparent and accountable governance. It's a calculated gamble, with potential high rewards if managed effectively.

Opportunities: The Silver Lining

Despite these challenges, road infrastructure development presents significant opportunities for countries like Zambia. By improving its road network, Zambia can stimulate economic growth, promote social inclusion, and enhance regional integration. Moreover, by adopting sustainable and inclusive approaches to infrastructure development, Zambia can ensure that the benefits of road infrastructure are widely shared and contribute to sustainable development. These opportunities are the silver lining, the potential rewards that make the challenges worth tackling.

In the following sections, we will get into these challenges and opportunities, exploring how Zambia can leverage road infrastructure development to drive economic growth and social development, while managing the associated risks and impacts. Let's navigate this path together, exploring the challenges and opportunities that lie ahead.

1.8 The Hidden Price: The Cost of Poor Road Infrastructure

The absence of a well-developed road infrastructure, or the presence of poorly maintained roads, can have substantial economic costs. These costs can manifest in various ways, impacting not just the economy but also the quality of life for individuals and communities. It's the hidden price we pay for neglecting our roads.

Increased Transportation Costs: The Slow Drain

Poor road conditions can significantly increase transportation costs. Roads in bad shape can slow down vehicles, leading to longer travel times and higher fuel consumption. This not only raises the cost of transporting goods, making products more expensive for consumers, but also increases the cost of commuting, reducing the disposable income of households. For businesses, these increased costs can erode their competitiveness, especially for those reliant on timely deliveries, like perishable goods suppliers or e-commerce platforms. It's a slow drain on the economy, siphoning off resources that could be used for growth and development.

Reduced Access to Markets and Services: The Invisible Barrier

A lack of adequate road infrastructure can also limit access to markets and services. For farmers and small businesses, poor roads can make it difficult to sell their products, reducing their income and growth potential. For consumers, it can limit access to goods and services, reducing their choices and increasing prices. Moreover, poor road connectivity can hinder access to essential services like education and healthcare, impacting human capital development and quality of life. It's an invisible barrier, holding back economic and social progress.

Deterred Investment: The Missed Opportunities

Poor road infrastructure can deter investment. Investors prefer locations with good infrastructure, as it reduces the cost and risk of doing business. Poor roads can increase the cost of transporting goods and services, reduce the reliability of deliveries, and limit access to markets and resources. This can make a region less attractive for investment, slowing down economic growth and job creation. It's a series of missed opportunities, hindering the potential for economic growth and development.

Increased Vehicle Maintenance and Accident Risks: The Unseen Dangers

Finally, poor road conditions can increase the cost of vehicle maintenance and the risk of accidents. Potholes, cracks, and other road damages can cause wear and tear on vehicles, leading to frequent repairs and replacements. This increases the cost of owning and operating a vehicle, impacting both businesses and households. Moreover, poor road conditions can increase the risk of accidents, leading to loss of life, injuries, and property damage. The economic cost of these accidents can be substantial, not to mention the human suffering they cause. It's the unseen dangers, lurking on every poorly maintained road.

In summary, while good road infrastructure can boost economic development, poor road infrastructure can have the opposite effect. It can increase costs, reduce access, deter investment, and increase the risk of accidents. Therefore, investing in road infrastructure is not just about building new roads; it's also about maintaining and improving existing ones. In the next sections, we will explore how this can be achieved and what it means for Zambia's economic future. Let's uncover the hidden price of poor road infrastructure and find ways to overcome these challenges.

1.9 The Unsung Hero: The Importance of Road Maintenance

Investing in road maintenance is a critical aspect of road economics that often does not receive the attention it deserves. Regular and timely maintenance can prevent roads from deteriorating, extending their lifespan, and ensuring they continue to serve their vital economic function. The economic returns from such investment can be substantial, yet it is frequently overlooked due to a variety of factors. It's the unsung hero of our road networks.

Cost-Effectiveness: The Penny Saved

One of the primary reasons for investing in road maintenance is its cost-effectiveness. It is far cheaper to maintain a road in good condition than to repair or rebuild it once it has deteriorated. Regular maintenance, such as filling potholes, sealing cracks, and resurfacing roads, can prevent minor issues from escalating into major problems that require expensive repairs. Moreover, well-maintained roads reduce vehicle operating costs and the risk of accidents, providing additional economic benefits. It's the penny saved that can lead to a pound earned.

Preventing Deterioration: The Stitch in Time

Roads are exposed to a variety of stresses, including traffic loads, weather conditions, and natural wear and tear. Without regular maintenance, these stresses can cause roads to deteriorate rapidly. This deterioration not only increases the cost of repairs but also reduces the functionality of roads. It can slow down traffic, increase transportation costs, and reduce access to markets and services. By investing in maintenance, we can prevent this deterioration and ensure that roads continue to contribute to economic development. It's the stitch in time that saves nine.

Overcoming Budget and Political Constraints: The Long View

Despite the clear benefits of road maintenance, it is often overlooked due to budget constraints and short-term political considerations. Maintenance budgets are often the first to be cut when resources are scarce, as the benefits of maintenance are less visible than those of new construction projects. Moreover, politicians may prefer to invest in new roads, which can be more appealing to voters than maintaining existing ones. However, this short-term thinking can lead to higher costs in the long run. It is therefore crucial to advocate for adequate maintenance budgets and to promote a long-term perspective on road infrastructure investment. It's the long view that ensures sustainable development.

In conclusion, road maintenance is a vital component of road infrastructure development. It is cost-effective, prevents road deterioration, and can yield high economic returns. However, to realize these benefits, we need to overcome the budget and political constraints that often hinder investment in maintenance. In the following sections, we will explore how this can be achieved, drawing on best practices and lessons learned from around the world. Let's sing the praises of the unsung hero of our road networks.

1.10 Lessons from the Road: Case Studies in Road Economics

In Chapter 8, we will be delving into a series of compelling case studies that highlight the profound economic impact of road infrastructure. These real-world examples, drawn from diverse countries and contexts, will serve to illustrate the transformative power of well-planned and well-executed road infrastructure projects. They will demonstrate how strategic investments in roads can catalyze economic growth and development, fostering prosperity and improving lives.

Each case study will provide a unique lens through which to view road economics, shedding light on different aspects of road infrastructure development. We will explore how roads have facilitated trade and connectivity, stimulated investment and job creation, and enhanced access to markets and services. We will also examine how countries have navigated the challenges associated with road infrastructure development, such as financing, maintenance, and environmental impact.

For instance, we might journey through the construction of the Interstate Highway System in the United States in the mid-20th century, which revolutionized the country's economy, fostering interstate trade and enabling the growth of industries like automobile manufacturing and retail. Alternatively, we could traverse the development of rural roads in China, which has played a pivotal role in lifting millions of people out of poverty by connecting remote rural areas to markets and services.

These case studies will not only provide valuable insights into the economic benefits of road infrastructure but also offer lessons that can be applied to the Zambian context. They will underscore the importance of factors such as policy planning, financing mechanisms, and maintenance strategies, which are crucial for the successful implementation of road infrastructure projects.

In subsequent chapters, we will take these principles and apply them to the specific context of Zambia. We will conduct a detailed examination of the current state of Zambia's road network, identifying its strengths and weaknesses. We will then explore the potential benefits of improving this network, from boosting economic productivity to enhancing social inclusion. Finally, we will discuss the challenges that need to be overcome, such as securing financing, ensuring sustainable maintenance, and balancing infrastructure development with environmental conservation. Through this exploration, we aim to chart a path forward for Zambia, one that leverages the power of road infrastructure to drive economic growth and prosperity. Let's learn from these lessons from the road and apply them to our journey towards prosperity.

Reflection and Action Plan:

As we draw this chapter to a close, I invite you to consider the economic implications of road infrastructure within your own locality. How does the current state of your roads influence the local economy and the prosperity of businesses in your area?

Reflection

Contemplate the question: In what ways does the condition of roads in your community impact local businesses and the overall economy? Consider factors such as accessibility, ease of transportation, and the potential for growth and development.

Action Plan

Take the initiative to learn more about the economic dynamics in your community. Engage with local business owners, community leaders, or economic development agencies to understand their perspectives on the role of road infrastructure in economic growth. Consider how you can contribute to discussions and actions aimed at improving road infrastructure for the economic benefit of your community. Remember, your voice and actions can contribute to the collective progress of your community.

2

ZAMBIA'S ROAD NETWORK

A Comprehensive Analysis

"The first lesson of economics is scarcity: there is never enough of anything to fully satisfy all those who want it. The first lesson of politics is to disregard the first lesson of economics." - Thomas Sowell.

In this chapter, we shift our focus to the core of Zambia's transportation system - its road network. We undertake an in-depth analysis of this crucial infrastructure, spotlighting its strengths and pinpointing areas that demand immediate enhancement. This evaluation will offer a lucid understanding of the challenges and opportunities that await Zambia as it seeks to harness its road network for economic development.

We initiate our exploration with an overview of Zambia's road network. We scrutinize the scope and quality of the network, considering factors such as road density, pavement condition, and bridge integrity. We also examine the geographical distribution of roads, acknowledging disparities between urban and rural areas, and between different regions of the country. This overview will underscore the strengths of Zambia's road network, such as its extensive coverage and the existence of well-maintained highways, while also drawing attention to areas of concern, such as the poor condition of many rural roads and the lack of connectivity in some remote areas.

Following this, we shift our focus to the influence of the road network on Zambia's trucking industry. As a landlocked country, Zambia heavily depends on road transport for both domestic and international trade. Trucks transport a wide array of goods across the country, from agricultural produce to imported commodities. The efficiency and competitiveness of this industry are directly linked to the state of the road network. We will investigate how road conditions affect the trucking industry, considering issues such as travel times, vehicle operating costs, and accident rates. This analysis will underscore the economic importance of good road infrastructure and the costs of neglecting it.

Finally, we consider the potential benefits of investing in road infrastructure. Drawing on the principles of road economics discussed in the previous chapter, we will investigate how enhancing Zambia's road network could boost economic productivity, enhance connectivity, and attract investment. We will also consider the potential social benefits, such as improved access to markets and services, and the potential environmental benefits, such as reduced vehicle emissions.

Throughout this chapter, we will utilize a wealth of data, research, and case studies to provide a comprehensive and nuanced picture of Zambia's road network. Our aim is to equip policymakers, stakeholders, and the general public with the information they need to make informed decisions about road infrastructure development in Zambia. By understanding the current state of the road network and the potential benefits of improving it, we can chart a path towards a more prosperous and inclusive future for Zambia.

2.1 An In-Depth Look at Zambia's Road Network

Zambia's road network, the lifeblood of the nation's transportation system, is a vital part of its economic framework. This intricate network weaves together the country's ten provinces, enabling the flow of goods, services, and people across its varied landscapes. However, the quality of this network is not consistent across the board, with certain regions benefiting from well-maintained roads while others contend with subpar infrastructure.

The road network forms the spine of Zambia's transportation system, acting as the primary conduit for domestic freight and passenger transport. It bridges the gap between urban hubs and rural locales, enabling access to markets, services, and opportunities. Furthermore, it connects Zambia with its eight neighboring countries, playing a crucial role in regional trade.

The trucking industry, a significant contributor to Zambia's economy, is heavily dependent on this road network. Trucks transport a diverse array of goods across the country, from agricultural produce harvested from rural farms to imported commodities destined for urban markets. This industry forms a critical link in Zambia's supply chain, bolstering sectors from agriculture and mining to manufacturing and retail.

However, the efficiency and productivity of the trucking industry, and by extension the broader economy, are intrinsically tied to the condition of the road network. Substandard road conditions can lead to a multitude of problems. Delays due to road repairs or challenging driving conditions can disrupt the timely delivery of goods, impacting both businesses and consumers. Increased operational costs, such as elevated fuel consumption and vehicle maintenance costs, can eat into the profits of trucking companies and inflate the cost of goods. Furthermore, poor road conditions can heighten the risk of accidents, leading to loss of life, damage to goods, and additional costs.

In certain regions of Zambia, the road network is well-developed and well-maintained, fostering efficient transportation and economic activity. However, in other areas, particularly in rural and remote regions, the infrastructure is lacking. Roads may be unpaved or poorly maintained, making transportation challenging, especially during the rainy season. These disparities in road infrastructure can lead to regional imbalances in economic development, with areas with poor road infrastructure often falling behind.

The image below shows a detailed review of the current main and secondary roads in Zambia and how they are inadequately distributed, leaving out huge chunks of the country:

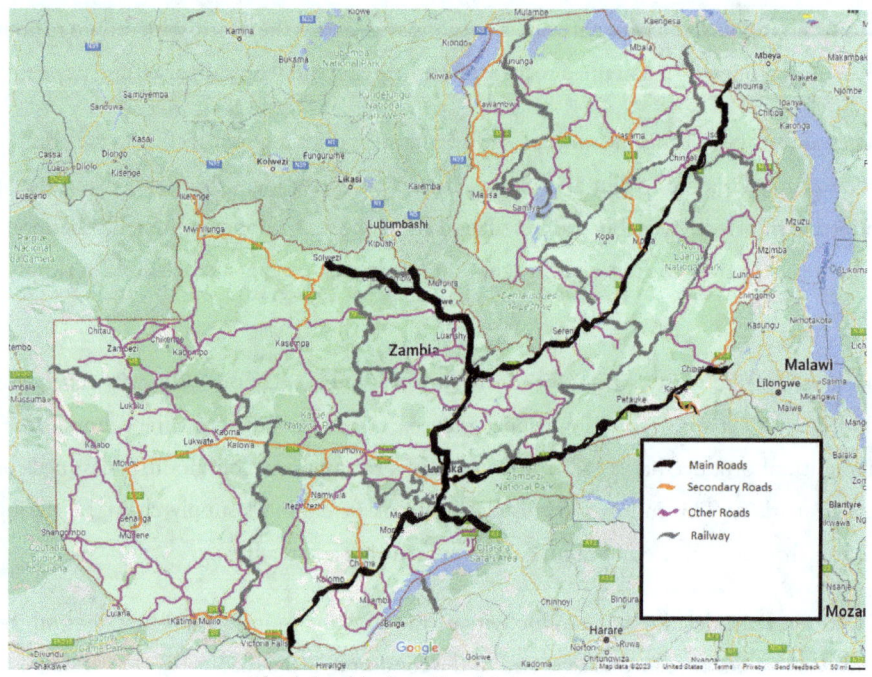

A high-level look at Zambia's main roads

In summary, Zambia's road network plays an indispensable role in the country's economy, supporting the movement of goods and services and facilitating economic activity. However, the varying quality of this network across the country presents significant challenges. In the subsequent sections, we will look further at these issues, exploring the impact of road infrastructure on Zambia's economy and examining potential solutions to these challenges.

2.2 Navigating Zambia's Geographic Landscape

Zambia's geographic positioning as a landlocked nation nestled in the heart of Southern Africa significantly shapes the role and importance of its road network. Enclosed by eight countries, Zambia's road network acts as a vital conduit for goods entering and exiting various neighboring nations, positioning it as a potential epicenter for regional trade.

This strategic positioning offers a unique opportunity for Zambia to function as a regional transportation hub. With a well-developed and well-maintained road network, Zambia could streamline the movement of goods across the region, enhancing trade and promoting regional integration. This could stimulate economic activity within Zambia, as transportation services, logistics, and related industries could flourish. It could also elevate Zambia's appeal as an investment destination, as businesses often favor locations with robust connectivity.

However, this strategic positioning also presents significant challenges. As a junction point for cross-border traffic, Zambia's road network must be equipped to manage substantial volumes of traffic. This necessitates not only a sufficient number of roads but also a high standard of infrastructure. Roads must be well-constructed and well-maintained to endure the wear and tear of heavy vehicles and to ensure reliable transportation under various weather conditions.

Furthermore, the cross-border nature of traffic introduces an additional layer of complexity to road infrastructure management. It demands effective coordination with neighboring countries on matters such as road standards, traffic regulations, and border controls. It also calls for measures to manage the environmental and social impacts of increased traffic, such as air pollution, noise, and road safety issues.

In addition, Zambia's varied geographical terrain, spanning from flat plains to mountainous regions, introduces its own set of challenges for road construction and maintenance. Different terrains necessitate different types of roads and maintenance strategies, adding to the complexity and cost of road infrastructure development.

In summary, while Zambia's geography offers opportunities, it also presents significant challenges for its road network. To leverage its strategic position and diverse terrain, Zambia needs to invest in developing a robust, resilient, and efficient road network. This will demand careful planning, sufficient financing, and effective management. In the subsequent sections, we will explore how this can be achieved, drawing on best practices and lessons learned from other countries.

2.3 Navigating the Challenges of Zambia's Road Network

Despite its strategic potential, Zambia's road network grapples with a myriad of challenges that impede its capacity to fully bolster the country's economic ambitions. These challenges span from issues of maintenance and coverage to capacity and efficiency, each presenting its unique set of complexities.

Maintenance Deficiencies: One of the most pressing issues plaguing Zambia's road network is inadequate maintenance. As discussed in Chapter 1, regular and timely maintenance is vital to maintain roads in optimal condition and prolong their lifespan. However, due to budget constraints, lack of technical expertise, or other factors, many roads in Zambia suffer from neglect. This neglect leads to rapid deterioration of road surfaces, escalating the risk of accidents and vehicle damage, and reducing the efficiency of transportation. Over time, the cost of rehabilitating these roads can far exceed the cost of regular maintenance, placing an additional burden on the country's resources.

Rural Coverage Shortfalls: While Zambia's road network is relatively extensive, its coverage is uneven, with rural areas often underserved. This lack of connectivity hampers economic development in these areas, limiting access to markets, services, and opportunities. It also exacerbates social inequalities, as rural populations may be cut off from essential services such as healthcare and education. Expanding road coverage in rural areas is therefore a critical challenge that needs to be addressed.

Capacity Constraints: With increasing economic activity and urbanization, Zambia's road network is facing growing pressure to handle increasing traffic volumes. Many roads, particularly in urban areas, are struggling to cope with the demand, leading to congestion, delays, and increased pollution. There is a need for significant upgrades, not just in terms of expanding the network, but also in improving the quality of roads, enhancing safety features, and incorporating modern traffic management systems.

Cross-Border Traffic Efficiency: As a landlocked country surrounded by eight neighbors, a significant portion of Zambia's road traffic is cross-border. However, the efficiency of this traffic is often hampered by delays at border crossings. These delays can be due to inadequate road infrastructure, cumbersome customs procedures, or lack of coordination between neighboring countries. Improving the efficiency of cross-border traffic requires not only improved road infrastructure, but also streamlined border processes and effective regional cooperation.

While Zambia's road network has the potential to significantly boost the country's economic development, realizing this potential requires addressing a range of challenges. In the upcoming sections, we will explore potential strategies for overcoming these challenges, drawing on best practices and lessons learned from other countries. Through a combination of improved maintenance, expanded coverage, capacity upgrades, and enhanced efficiency, Zambia can transform its road network into a powerful engine of economic growth and prosperity.

However, the quality and impact of road infrastructure are not just measured in terms of physical condition or economic benefits. Road safety, particularly the issue of road traffic accidents, is a crucial aspect of social responsibility that needs to be addressed, and we look at this issue next.

2.4 Road Safety and Social Responsibility: Tackling the Traffic Accident Crisis

Road traffic accidents pose a significant public health and safety threat in Zambia, with the country's high road fatality rate ranking among the highest globally. This alarming statistic underscores the urgent need for comprehensive interventions. Addressing this issue transcends the realm of infrastructure development, extending into the sphere of *social responsibility*.

Narrow road sharing heavy transport vehicles and local traffic

The state of Zambia's roads significantly contributes to these accidents. Common infrastructural deficiencies such as potholes, uneven surfaces, and lack of road markings present navigational challenges for drivers, increasing the likelihood of accidents. These infrastructural issues highlight the importance of investing in road maintenance and upgrades, not merely for efficiency and economic growth, but crucially for the safety of road users.

However, infrastructure improvements alone cannot fully address the problem. The high incidence of traffic accidents in Zambia also points to behavioral issues. The lack of enforcement of traffic laws and widespread disregard for them by drivers lead to dangerous driving behaviors such as speeding, drunk driving, and reckless driving. This situation underscores the need for effective law enforcement, complemented by education and awareness campaigns to promote safe driving habits.

Road shared by pedestrians and vehicles both large and small

In 2017, the Zambian government initiated the "***Zambia: Safe on Roads***" campaign to raise awareness about road safety issues and encourage safer driving. While this is a commendable step, more sustained and comprehensive efforts are needed. These could include stricter law enforcement, regular driver education programs, and initiatives to promote vehicle maintenance.

Furthermore, the high road fatality rate in Zambia is not just a national concern but a regional one. As Zambia serves as a key node in several major transport corridors in Southern Africa, road safety in Zambia has implications for the wider region. Therefore, improving road safety in Zambia could contribute to safer and more efficient transport networks across Southern Africa.

In conclusion, addressing the issue of road traffic accidents in Zambia requires a multi-faceted approach encompassing infrastructure development, law enforcement, education, and regional cooperation. By tackling this challenge, Zambia can not only enhance the safety and well-being of its own citizens but also contribute to a safer and more integrated Southern Africa.

2.5 Road Safety and Sustainable Development: Aligning with Global Targets

Road safety is an integral aspect of sustainable development, with road infrastructure playing a pivotal role in fostering safer roads. Well-designed and well-maintained roads can significantly reduce the occurrence of road traffic accidents. However, defects or deficiencies in the road infrastructure can disrupt the balance and safety margins that ensure the proper functioning of the system, thereby increasing the risk of accidents.

The World Health Organization (WHO) has highlighted the negative impact of unsafe vehicles and unsafe road infrastructure on road safety. In line with this, the 2030 Agenda for Sustainable Development includes specific targets addressing road safety. Target 3.6 aims to halve global road traffic deaths and injuries by 2030, while Target 11.2 aims to provide access to safe, affordable, accessible, and sustainable transport systems for all, with a particular emphasis on improving road safety.

These targets underscore the importance of investing in road infrastructure not just for the sake of economic development, but also for the safety and well-being of road users. For Zambia, this means that efforts to improve the road network must also prioritize safety features such as clear road markings, adequate signage, and well-designed intersections. It also means that road maintenance should not only focus on preserving the physical condition of the roads, but also on ensuring their safety features remain effective.

Moreover, the emphasis on 'sustainable transport systems' in Target 11.2 highlights the need for Zambia to consider the environmental impact of its road network. This includes considering how road construction and maintenance practices can minimize environmental harm, and how the road network can support more sustainable modes of transport, such as public transportation and non-motorized transport.

In conclusion, addressing the issue of road safety in Zambia requires a comprehensive approach that integrates safety considerations into all aspects of road infrastructure development and management. By doing so, Zambia can not only reduce road traffic accidents and meet its commitments under the 2030 Agenda, but also create a road network that supports sustainable and inclusive development.

2.6 Economic Implications of Zambia's Road Network: Lessons from Global Experiences

The state and extent of Zambia's road network hold significant implications for the country's economic trajectory. To elucidate this point, we can draw insights from research conducted on China's truck market and the transformative impact of highway infrastructure on its growth.

China embarked on an ambitious highway construction program in the late 20th century, resulting in one of the world's most extensive and well-maintained road networks. This robust infrastructure has facilitated the efficient movement of goods across the vast country, underpinning the growth of domestic and international trade, and providing a significant boost to the economy.

The trucking industry, in particular, has reaped substantial benefits from this improved infrastructure. Enhanced road conditions have enabled trucks to travel faster and more reliably, reducing transportation costs and bolstering the competitiveness of the industry. This, in turn, has spurred growth in sectors such as manufacturing, retail, and e-commerce, which heavily rely on trucking for their supply chains.

Moreover, the expansive highway network has unlocked remote and previously inaccessible areas, fostering regional development and mitigating economic disparities. It has also attracted investment, both domestic and foreign, by improving the business environment and enhancing the profitability of investments.

Drawing parallels from China's experience, Zambia, with its vast and diverse landscape and significant regional disparities in economic development, stands to gain immensely from an expanded and improved road network. Enhanced connectivity could facilitate the movement of goods and people across the country, stimulating trade, connectivity, and social inclusion.

For the trucking industry, superior roads could lower operating costs, improve reliability, and expand market access. This could catalyze the growth of the industry and stimulate economic activity in sectors that rely on trucking. Furthermore, it could attract investment by improving the business environment and enhancing the profitability of investments.

However, it's crucial to note that the benefits of road infrastructure are not automatic. They hinge on a range of factors, including the quality of the roads, the efficiency of the trucking industry, and the policy environment. In the subsequent sections, we will again delve deeper into these factors, examining how Zambia can leverage its road network for sustainable economic development.

2.7 Transforming Challenges into Opportunities: Pathways for Enhancing Zambia's Road Network

While Zambia's road network faces considerable challenges, these hurdles can be transformed into catalysts for economic growth. Several opportunities exist that leverage Zambia's unique attributes, innovative financing mechanisms, and lessons gleaned from successful global examples.

Capitalizing on Strategic Location

Zambia's strategic location, landlocked and surrounded by eight countries, presents a unique opportunity. By enhancing its road network, Zambia can position itself as a regional transportation hub, facilitating the movement of goods across Southern Africa. This could stimulate trade, attract investment, and spur economic growth. Moreover, it could bolster Zambia's geopolitical influence, enabling it to play a more active role in regional integration efforts.

Exploring Innovative Financing Mechanisms

Financing poses a significant challenge for road infrastructure development. However, Zambia could explore innovative financing mechanisms to overcome this hurdle. These include public-private partnerships, where private entities invest in road construction in return for a share of the revenues; road funds, where a portion of fuel taxes or vehicle registration fees is earmarked for road maintenance; and development finance, where international development institutions provide loans or grants for infrastructure projects. These mechanisms could supplement government funding, enabling Zambia to invest in its road network without straining its fiscal resources.

Drawing Lessons from Successful Global Examples

Numerous countries have successfully improved their road networks, and Zambia can draw valuable lessons from their experiences. These countries have adopted a range of strategies, from prioritizing maintenance to decentralizing road management, and from promoting road safety to mitigating environmental impacts. By studying these examples, Zambia can identify best practices and avoid common pitfalls in road infrastructure development.

Investing in Road Network Enhancement

Investing in its road network can yield significant dividends for Zambia. It can enhance the efficiency of its trucking industry, facilitate the movement of goods and people, and drive economic growth. Improved roads can reduce transportation costs, improve reliability, and expand market access. They can also attract investment, stimulate tourism, and enhance social inclusion. The benefits of road infrastructure investment, both direct and indirect, can be substantial.

In the subsequent chapters, we will delve deeper into these issues. We will examine the potential impact of road infrastructure on Zambia's GDP, exploring how improved roads can boost economic productivity and foster development. We will also explore financing options for road infrastructure, discussing how Zambia can mobilize the resources needed for this critical investment. Finally, we will discuss how Zambia can balance infrastructure development with other national priorities, ensuring that road development contributes to sustainable and inclusive growth. Through this exploration, we aim to provide a roadmap for improving Zambia's road network and unlocking its economic potential.

Reflection and Action Plan

As we conclude this chapter, I encourage you to take a moment to reflect on the state of the roads in your own community. How do they compare to the ideal we've discussed in this chapter? What improvements could be made, and how would these changes impact your daily life and the lives of those around you?

Reflection:

Identify the most pressing road infrastructure issues in your community. Are they related to the quality of the roads, traffic management, or perhaps safety measures?

Action Plan:

Consider how you, as an individual or as part of a community, can contribute to addressing these issues. Could you raise awareness about these problems, advocate for change at the local government level, or participate in community initiatives aimed at improving road infrastructure? Remember, every journey begins with a single step, and every change starts with an idea. Your actions can make a difference.

3

SAFEGUARDING THE HIGHWAYS

The Imperative of Security in Road Infrastructure Development

"Good, reliable transportation systems are crucial to a nation's defense and its economy. They are the lifelines of our modern civilization." - Dwight D. Eisenhower, 34th President of the United States and advocate for the U.S. Interstate Highway System.

In the previous chapter, we delved into the current state of Zambia's road network, highlighting its pivotal role in the nation's economic fabric. Now, we shift our focus to a critical yet often underappreciated aspect of road infrastructure: security. Woven into the intricate tapestry of road infrastructure development, security serves as a silent yet potent force. As we journey along the highways to prosperity, it's paramount to ensure these pathways are not only efficient and well-maintained but also secure. This chapter delves into the significance of security in road infrastructure, with a particular emphasis on cargo transportation. We will explore the challenges, the current measures, and the innovative solutions that are shaping the future of secure road transportation in Zambia. By understanding the security landscape, we can better appreciate the complexities involved in managing and developing our road network.

In the grand scheme of economic development, the security of road infrastructure plays a pivotal role. It is the invisible shield that safeguards the flow of goods, services, and people. It is the silent sentinel that protects our investments, our livelihoods, and our aspirations. Without it, the highways to prosperity could quickly turn into pathways of loss and disruption.

In Zambia, a country where road transport forms the backbone of commerce and connectivity, the importance of road security is magnified. With a vast network of roads stretching across diverse terrains and linking numerous economic hubs, the task of ensuring secure transportation is both challenging and crucial.

In this chapter, we will navigate the complex terrain of road security. We will look at the challenges that loom large, from theft and vandalism to accidents and infrastructure damage. We will explore the measures that are currently in place to mitigate these risks, from physical security protocols to advanced technological solutions.

But our journey does not stop there. We will also venture into the realm of innovation, exploring how companies like VS Cargo Ltd are pioneering new approaches to secure cargo management. Through their lens, we will gain insights into the future of secure road transportation in Zambia - a future where security is not just an afterthought, but a fundamental pillar of infrastructure development.

So, buckle up as we set off on this journey. It's time to shine a spotlight on the vital role of security in road infrastructure development and explore how it shapes our journey on the highways to prosperity.

In the context of Zambia, where road transport is the backbone of commerce and connectivity, the importance of road security is magnified. With a vast network of roads stretching across diverse terrains and linking numerous economic hubs, the task of ensuring secure transportation is both challenging and crucial. This chapter will delve into the challenges that loom large, from theft and vandalism to accidents and infrastructure damage. We will explore the measures that are currently in place to mitigate these risks, from physical security protocols to advanced technological solutions.

However, our journey does not stop there. We will also venture into the realm of innovation, exploring how companies like VS Cargo Ltd are pioneering new approaches to secure cargo management. Through their lens, we will gain insights into the future of secure road transportation in Zambia - a future where security is not just an afterthought, but a fundamental pillar of infrastructure development.

As we set off on this journey, we will shine a spotlight on the vital role of security in road infrastructure development and explore how it shapes our journey on the highways to prosperity. We will also consider the broader implications of road security, from its impact on economic development and social equity to its role in achieving the Sustainable Development Goals. By understanding the security landscape, we can better appreciate the complexities involved in managing and developing our road network and envision a future where our highways are not just pathways to prosperity, but also corridors of safety and security.

3.1 Navigating the Security Terrain: Understanding the Challenges

Road transportation, especially in the domain of cargo transportation, is a landscape fraught with security challenges. These challenges take various forms, from the theft of goods during transit to vandalism of vehicles and infrastructure. Damage due to poor road conditions or accidents also poses a significant risk, often leading to costly delays and repairs.

These incidents are not merely isolated losses; they create ripples, disrupting supply chains, causing businesses to suffer, and impacting the broader economy. The effects can be particularly detrimental in a country like Zambia, where road transport is the backbone of cargo movement, connecting businesses to markets and facilitating the flow of goods both within and beyond the country's borders.

In this context, addressing security challenges becomes not just a matter of preventing individual losses, but a crucial step towards ensuring the smooth functioning of the entire economic system. It's about creating an environment where businesses can operate with confidence, where goods can be transported efficiently and safely, and where the benefits of road infrastructure can be fully realized.

In the following sections, we will get into these security challenges, exploring their implications in more detail and examining the measures that can be taken to mitigate them. This will include a look at both physical security measures and technological solutions, providing a comprehensive overview of the strategies available for enhancing security in road transportation.

We will also consider the broader implications of these challenges, including their impact on Zambia's economic development and social equity, as well as their relevance to the Sustainable Development Goals. By understanding the security landscape, we can better appreciate the complexities involved in managing and developing our road network and envision a future where our highways are not just pathways to prosperity, but also corridors of safety and security.

3.2 Fortifying the Highways: Security Measures in Road Infrastructure

Securing road infrastructure is a complex task that necessitates a comprehensive, multi-layered approach. It involves not only the physical protection of the infrastructure itself but also the safeguarding of the goods and people that traverse these roads.

Physical security measures form the first line of defense. This includes the installation of robust fencing around critical infrastructure to deter unauthorized access. Adequate lighting is another crucial element, as well-lit roads can deter criminal activities and enhance visibility for drivers, thereby reducing the risk of accidents. Secure rest stops along major highways provide safe havens for long-haul truckers, protecting both the drivers and their cargo during necessary breaks.

On the technological front, the advent of digital tools has revolutionized security in road transportation. Tracking systems, for instance, allow for real-time monitoring of vehicles, providing valuable data that can aid in the quick recovery of stolen goods and the apprehension of culprits. Secure communication channels enable efficient coordination between drivers, fleet managers, and security personnel, facilitating swift responses to any security incidents.

Moreover, the integration of Artificial Intelligence (AI) and Machine Learning (ML) technologies is opening new frontiers in road security. From predictive analytics that can identify potential threats to advanced surveillance systems that can detect unusual activities, these technologies are set to play a pivotal role in the future of road security.

However, the implementation of these measures is not without challenges. It requires significant investment, a well-trained workforce, and a regulatory environment that supports the adoption of new technologies. In the following sections, we will venture further into these issues, exploring the practicalities of implementing security measures in road infrastructure and discussing potential strategies for overcoming the challenges.

We will also consider the role of policy and regulation in enhancing road security, examining how government action can support the adoption of these measures and foster a culture of security in road transportation. By weaving together physical security measures, technological innovations, and supportive policies, we can create a robust security framework that protects our road infrastructure and ensures the safe and efficient movement of goods and people.

3.3 VS Cargo Ltd – A Vanguard in Secure Cargo Management

One company that stands at the forefront of secure cargo management in Zambia is VS Cargo Ltd. With a keen focus on providing real-time solutions for cargo safety, VS Cargo Ltd has been instrumental in securing high-value cargo from the point of collection to their ports of exit.

Established in 1997, VS Cargo Ltd has been a trailblazer in the logistics and warehousing industry in Zambia. The company was the first to initiate the transshipment model in the Copperbelt region, setting the stage for a robust logistics hub. With a vision to handle rail and road logistics inwards and outwards of the Democratic Republic of Congo, as well as various countries in the Sub-Saharan Region, VS Cargo Ltd has been instrumental in shaping the logistics landscape of Zambia.

The company's warehousing facility, located in the heart of Ndola's Industrial area, is equipped with state-of-the-art CCTV surveillance systems, a parking facility for over 100 trucks, and a dual rail siding capable of handling block trains. The facility also includes specialized cold-room storage for food or chemical goods and bagging equipment for break bulk requirements.

VS Cargo Ltd's commitment to secure cargo management began in 2009, with the aim to provide real-time solutions for cargo safety in transit across their region of operations. The company ensures that high-value cargo is secured from the point of collection up to their ports of exit. This focus on security has made VS Cargo Ltd a leader in secure cargo management in Zambia.

The company's services extend beyond warehousing and logistics. VS Cargo Ltd also offers customs clearing and freight forwarding services through its subsidiary company, iClearX-press. With offices located across Zambia's border posts, the company is well-positioned to handle documentation requirements for cargo transiting in and out of Zambia.

In addition to these services, VS Cargo Ltd has a dedicated security department that manages an average monthly capacity of 25 to 50,000 tons. The department operates 24/7 and has 16 checkpoints across Zambia, DRC, Tanzania, and Zimbabwe. This comprehensive approach to cargo management, combined with their pioneering spirit, makes VS Cargo Ltd a key player in Zambia's road infrastructure development.

VS Cargo Ltd's innovative approach to secure cargo management serves as a model for other companies in the industry. By integrating advanced security measures into their operations, they have demonstrated that it is possible to ensure the safe and efficient movement of goods, even in challenging environments. Their success underscores the potential of secure cargo management to boost economic growth and development in Zambia.

3.4 Case Study - VS Cargo Ltd: A Hypothetical Exploration

In this section, we delve into a hypothetical exploration of strategies that could be employed by VS Cargo Ltd. We consider the challenges they've likely faced, the innovative solutions they could implement, and the potential outcomes of such an approach. This case study provides a practical perspective on the intersection of road infrastructure and security.

VS Cargo Ltd, established in 1997, has been a pioneer in handling rail and road logistics in and out of the Democratic Republic of Congo and various countries in the Sub-Saharan Region. Particularly noteworthy is their focus on the security aspect of cargo management, a crucial element in the logistics and transportation industry.

Probable Challenges

In the complex landscape of road logistics, VS Cargo Ltd likely faces numerous challenges. Ensuring the safety of high-value cargo across vast geographical areas is no easy task. Threats of theft or damage to cargo, potential corruption, and unpredictable road conditions could pose significant risks. Additionally, coordinating with various stakeholders, including customs and border control, police, and local authorities, could also present logistical and administrative challenges.

Hypothetical Strategies

To overcome these challenges, VS Cargo Ltd would need to implement robust security measures. This could include the use of advanced tracking systems to monitor cargo in real-time, ensuring immediate response to any incidents. Furthermore, partnerships with local law enforcement agencies could enhance security efforts, allowing for swift action when required.

They might also employ rigorous staff training and strict operating procedures to minimize human error and deter any potential internal threats. To manage the complexities of cross-border operations, VS Cargo Ltd could also develop a strong network of local contacts and partners to facilitate smoother operations.

Potential Innovative Solutions

In a bid to provide real-time solutions for cargo safety, VS Cargo Ltd could leverage digital technologies. For instance, Internet of Things (IoT) sensors could provide detailed data on cargo conditions and location. AI-powered predictive analytics could help anticipate potential risks and suggest optimal routes for transportation.

Anticipated Outcomes and Impact

By implementing these strategies, VS Cargo Ltd could significantly enhance the security of its cargo operations. This would not only protect their clients' interests but also potentially reduce insurance costs and increase operational efficiency. Furthermore, by pioneering these security measures, VS Cargo Ltd could set industry standards and influence policy discussions around road infrastructure and security. This hypothetical exploration underscores the potential of innovative security measures in transforming the road logistics industry.

3.5 The Role of Security in Infrastructure Development

The necessity of secure cargo transportation has profound implications for the design, development, and maintenance of road infrastructure. Security considerations can influence a multitude of factors, from the selection of routes to the positioning of rest stops, and the integration of smart technologies.

Security considerations can dictate the choice of routes for road development. For instance, routes that pass through areas with a high incidence of theft or vandalism may be avoided in favor of safer alternatives. This can lead to the development of new roads in areas that were previously underserved, potentially opening up new opportunities for economic development.

The placement of rest stops is another area where security considerations come into play. Rest stops are essential for long-haul truck drivers, providing them with a place to rest and refresh. However, these locations can also be hotspots for theft and other security incidents. Therefore, secure rest stops, equipped with adequate lighting, fencing, and surveillance systems, need to be strategically placed along the routes. This not only ensures the safety of the drivers and their cargo but also enhances the overall efficiency of the transportation system.

The adoption of smart technologies is another aspect of infrastructure development that is influenced by security needs. Technologies such as GPS tracking systems, secure communication channels, and advanced surveillance systems can significantly enhance the security of cargo transportation. These technologies can provide real-time monitoring of cargo, alert authorities to any security breaches, and even help in the recovery of stolen goods. The integration of these technologies into road infrastructure requires careful planning and investment.

Learning from the U.S. Model

Looking to the United States, we can see an example of a country that has effectively integrated security considerations into its infrastructure development. The U.S. Department of

Transportation has a dedicated Office of Intelligence, Security, and Emergency Response, which works to ensure the safety and security of the country's transportation system. They employ a range of strategies, from physical security measures to advanced technological solutions, to protect cargo and passengers.

For instance, the U.S. has implemented stringent regulations for cargo transportation, including mandatory background checks for commercial drivers, strict controls on the transportation of hazardous materials, and comprehensive safety inspections of commercial vehicles. They have also embraced technology, using electronic logging devices to monitor drivers' hours of service and prevent fatigue-related accidents, and advanced screening technologies to inspect cargo at ports and border crossings.

In terms of infrastructure design, the U.S. has adopted the concept of 'Crime Prevention Through Environmental Design' (CPTED), which uses design principles to reduce the likelihood of crime. This includes strategies such as improving visibility along roads and at rest stops, using physical barriers to control access, and ensuring regular maintenance to signal that an area is well-cared for and monitored.

These measures have not only enhanced the security of cargo transportation in the U.S. but have also contributed to the efficiency and reliability of the transportation system as a whole. They serve as a model for other countries, including Zambia, on how to integrate security considerations into infrastructure development.

In conclusion, the need for secure cargo transportation significantly influences infrastructure development. By integrating security considerations into the design and development of roads and related facilities, we can create a transportation system that is not only efficient and reliable but also safe and secure. This will be crucial for Zambia as it works to develop its road infrastructure and boost its economic growth.

3.6 Policy Recommendations for Enhancing Road Security

Drawing from the insights gathered from the case study of VS Cargo Ltd and the broader discussion on security in road infrastructure, we can formulate several recommendations for policymakers. These recommendations aim to bolster the security of road infrastructure, thereby enhancing the reliability and efficiency of road transportation in Zambia.

3.6.1 Invest in Physical Security Measures

Policymakers should prioritize investment in physical security measures. This includes secure rest stops, adequate lighting, and robust fencing along major transportation routes. These measures can significantly deter theft and vandalism, enhancing the security of cargo transportation.

3.6.2 Embrace Smart Technologies

The adoption and integration of smart technologies such as GPS tracking systems, secure communication channels, and advanced surveillance systems should be encouraged. These technologies can provide real-time monitoring of cargo, alert authorities to any security breaches, and even aid in the recovery of stolen goods.

3.6.3 Strengthen Legal and Regulatory Frameworks

There is a need for policymakers to work towards strengthening the legal and regulatory frameworks governing cargo transportation. This could include stricter penalties for theft and vandalism, mandatory background checks for commercial drivers, and stringent controls on the transportation of hazardous materials.

3.6.4 Promote Public-Private Partnerships

Public-private partnerships in the area of road infrastructure security should be encouraged. Private companies like VS Cargo Ltd have valuable expertise and resources that can be leveraged to enhance the security of road transportation.

3.6.5 Invest in Training and Capacity Building

Investment in training and capacity building for law enforcement agencies, transportation companies, and other stakeholders involved in cargo transportation is crucial. This can enhance their ability to prevent and respond to security incidents, thereby contributing to the overall security of the road infrastructure.

By implementing these recommendations, Zambia can significantly enhance the security of its road infrastructure, ensuring the safe and efficient movement of goods and people across the country. This will not only boost the reliability of the transportation system but also contribute to the country's economic growth and development.

3.7 Learning from Global Best Practices

As we strive to enhance the security of Zambia's road infrastructure, it is beneficial to look beyond our borders and learn from the experiences of other countries. Several developed nations have successfully tackled the issue of road security, providing valuable lessons that can be adapted to Zambia's context.

3.7.1 The United States Model

In the United States, the Department of Transportation collaborates closely with private companies, law enforcement agencies, and other stakeholders to ensure the security of cargo transportation. They have implemented stringent regulations, invested in advanced technologies, and promoted public-private partnerships to enhance security. Their comprehensive approach to road security has resulted in a robust and secure transportation system that supports the country's economic growth.

3.7.2 The European Union Approach

Similarly, in the European Union, the EU Transport Security Policy provides a comprehensive framework for ensuring the security of all modes of transportation, including road transportation. The policy includes measures such as risk assessments, security inspections, and training programs for transportation workers. This holistic approach has helped the EU maintain a high level of security across its vast and diverse transportation network.

3.7.3 Adapting to Zambia's Context

While the specific strategies used by the US and the EU may not be directly applicable to Zambia due to differences in resources, infrastructure, and regulatory environments, the underlying principles can certainly guide Zambia's efforts. The importance of collaboration between different stakeholders, the value of investing in advanced technologies, and the need for robust regulations and enforcement are universal lessons that can be adapted to Zambia's context.

In conclusion, enhancing the security of road infrastructure is a complex task that requires a comprehensive and multi-faceted approach. By adopting the right mix of physical security measures, smart technologies, legal and regulatory reforms, and public-private partnerships, Zambia can significantly enhance the security of its road infrastructure. This will not only boost the reliability and efficiency of road transportation but will also contribute to the country's economic development. As we move forward, it is crucial to keep learning, adapting, and innovating, drawing on both our own experiences and the lessons learned from others.

3.8 Securing the Path to Prosperity

As we conclude this chapter, we underscore the indispensable role of security in the broader narrative of road infrastructure development. The journey towards prosperity isn't merely about constructing roads or expanding networks; it's equally about ensuring these pathways are secure and reliable, fostering an environment where commerce and trade can flourish without undue risk.

The case of VS Cargo Ltd, a pioneer in secure cargo management in Zambia, serves as a testament to the transformative potential of integrating security measures into the fabric of road infrastructure. Their innovative approach to cargo safety, leveraging both physical and technological measures, offers valuable insights that can guide future infrastructure development.

In a country like Zambia, where road transport plays a significant role in the movement of goods and services, addressing security challenges isn't just a necessity—it's an imperative. It's about safeguarding the economic lifeline of the nation, protecting the interests of businesses, and ultimately, contributing to the nation's economic growth and development.

As Zambia continues to develop and expand its road network, the lessons gleaned from this chapter will be instrumental. They provide a roadmap for integrating security considerations into infrastructure planning and development, ensuring that as we build the highways to prosperity, we also build the safeguards that protect this journey.

The integration of security measures into road infrastructure development is a dynamic and ongoing process. It requires the concerted efforts of policymakers, infrastructure developers, security agencies, and the transportation industry. It's about creating a culture of security, where every stakeholder understands their role and responsibility in protecting the integrity of the road network.

In the end, *the goal is to create a road infrastructure that is not just expansive and efficient, but also secure and reliable.* A road network that supports the economic aspirations of Zambia, propelling the nation towards a prosperous future. As we continue this journey, let us remember that the roads to prosperity are not just about the destination—they're also about the journey, and ensuring that this journey is secure for all.

In the subsequent chapters, we will look further into the potential impact of road infrastructure on Zambia's GDP, exploring how improved roads can boost economic productivity and foster development. We will also explore financing options for road infrastructure, discussing how Zambia can mobilize the resources needed for this critical investment. Finally, we will discuss how Zambia can balance infrastructure development with other national priorities, ensuring that road development contributes to sustainable and inclusive growth. Through this exploration, we aim to provide a roadmap for improving Zambia's road network and unlocking its economic potential.

Reflection and Action Plan:

Reflection:

As you reach the end of this chapter, take a moment to reflect on the importance of security in road infrastructure
development. Think about the various security challenges
that exist and the measures that can be put in place to
mitigate these risks. Consider the case of VS Cargo Ltd and
how they have integrated security into their operations.
How does this example influence your understanding of the
role of security in road infrastructure?

Action Plan:

- **Research**: Look up more about the security measures
  in place in your local area or country. How do these
  compare to the measures discussed in this chapter?

- **Discussion**: Engage in a discussion with peers, col-
  leagues, or friends about the importance of security
  in road infrastructure. Share what you've learned
  from this chapter and listen to their perspectives.

- **Advocacy**: Consider ways you can advocate for better
  security in road infrastructure in your community.
  This could be through writing to local represen-
  tatives, participating in community meetings, or
  raising awareness through social media.

- **Future Learning**: Identify areas related to security
  in road infrastructure that you'd like to learn more
  about. This could be a specific security measure, a
  case study of a particular country, or the role of

technology in enhancing security.

- **Personal Impact**: Reflect on how the security of road infrastructure impacts your daily life. How would improvements in this area affect you personally?

Remember, the journey towards a secure and prosperous future is a collective one. Your understanding, engagement, and action can make a difference.

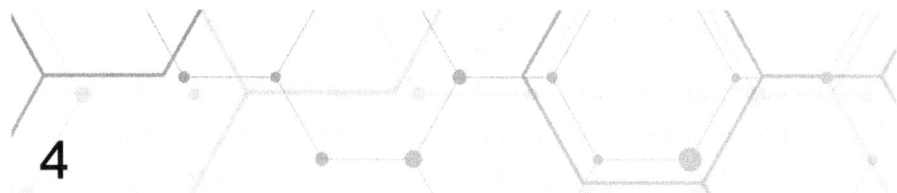

4

THE ECONOMIC LIFELINE

Unraveling the Impact of Road Infrastructure on GDP

"Investment in infrastructure is a long term requirement for growth and a long term factor that will make growth sustainable." - Jacob Zuma.

I n this chapter, we study the intricate tapestry of the relationship between road infrastructure and a nation's Gross Domestic Product (GDP), with a spotlight on Zambia. Our aim is to illuminate the profound ways in which the quality and extent of road infrastructure can shape a nation's economic trajectory, influencing diverse sectors and impacting overall productivity.

Road infrastructure is far more than a mere network of paths—it is a cornerstone of economic development. It enables the flow of goods and services, connects individuals to employment and markets, and underpins key sectors such as agriculture, manufacturing, and tourism. By enhancing connectivity and reducing transportation costs, a robust and well-maintained road network can significantly amplify a country's GDP.

We commence this exploration by offering a theoretical overview of the impact of road infrastructure on GDP. Drawing from economic theory and empirical research, we will unpack concepts such as the direct and indirect effects of infrastructure investment, the role of roads in enhancing productivity, and the multiplier effects of infrastructure spending.

Subsequently, we shift our focus to the Zambian landscape. We will conduct an in-depth analysis of how the current state of Zambia's road network is influencing its GDP. This will involve examining the effects on various sectors, such as agriculture, mining, and tourism, which are heavily reliant on road transport. We will also delve into the impact on the trucking industry, a vital cog in Zambia's domestic and international trade.

Following this, we will explore the potential benefits that could be reaped from enhancing Zambia's road network. Utilizing economic modeling and case study evidence, we will estimate the potential surge in GDP that could result from various infrastructure investments. This will paint a clear picture of the economic dividends that Zambia could garner from improving its road network.

In the final section, we will discuss the policy implications of our findings. We will contemplate how Zambia can leverage its road infrastructure to catalyze GDP growth, discussing issues such as investment priorities, financing mechanisms, and maintenance strategies. We will also consider how to strike a balance between the economic benefits of road development and social and environmental considerations, ensuring that infrastructure development contributes to sustainable and inclusive growth.

Through this exploration, we aim to provide a comprehensive understanding of the economic significance of road infrastructure. By highlighting the potential impact on GDP, we hope to underscore the urgency of investing in Zambia's road network and provide valuable insights to guide policy decisions.

4.1 Unraveling the Connection: Road Infrastructure and GDP

Road infrastructure, as a fundamental element of a country's physical capital, plays a decisive role in shaping economic productivity. It forms the spine of a nation's transportation system, influencing the efficiency and cost-effectiveness of trade, and ultimately impacting the Gross Domestic Product (GDP). The relationship between road infrastructure and GDP is complex, with roads contributing to economic productivity in numerous direct and indirect ways.

Enabling the Flow of Goods and Services

At its core, road infrastructure enables the flow of goods and services across a country. It connects producers to consumers, suppliers to manufacturers, and businesses to markets. This connectivity is vital for the functioning of an economy. Without an efficient road network, the movement of goods and services can become slow and costly, impeding trade and economic activity. On the other hand, a well-developed and well-maintained road network can facilitate trade, leading to increased economic productivity and a higher GDP.

Minimizing Transportation Costs

By enhancing the efficiency of transportation, robust road infrastructure can significantly reduce transportation costs. This includes not only the direct costs of transportation, such as fuel and vehicle maintenance, but also indirect costs, such as the time spent on the road. Lower transportation costs can increase the profitability of businesses, stimulate economic activity, and boost GDP. They can also lead to lower prices for consumers, increasing purchasing power and stimulating demand.

Broadening Access to Markets

Road infrastructure broadens access to markets, both domestically and internationally. For domestic markets, roads connect producers in rural areas with consumers in urban areas, enabling the exchange of goods and services. For international markets, roads connect businesses to ports, airports, and border crossings, facilitating exports and imports. By enhancing market access, road infrastructure can stimulate competition, foster specialization, and promote economic growth.

Beyond these direct effects, road infrastructure can also have indirect impacts on GDP. For instance, it can stimulate investment by improving the business environment, attract tourists by providing access to tourist sites, and enhance social inclusion by connecting remote areas to urban centers. It can also have multiplier effects, with the spending on road construction and maintenance stimulating economic activity in other sectors.

4.1.1 The Global Perspective: Transport Infrastructure and Economic Performance

As we look further into the impact of road infrastructure on GDP, it's crucial to note that this relationship isn't unique to Zambia or developing nations alone. A study conducted by researchers from the University of Antwerp and the University of Tokyo examined the relationship between transport infrastructure and performance in rail and road freight transport in Japan and selected European countries.

The study found a significant positive correlation between transport infrastructure and economic performance. This means that improvements in transport infrastructure, including road networks, were associated with increased economic performance. The researchers used a correlation coefficient to measure the strength of this relationship, with values closer to 1 indicating a stronger positive correlation.

The study also found that the correlation was particularly strong in countries with a high degree of urbanization, such as Japan and many European countries. This suggests that the benefits of transport infrastructure investment may be even greater in densely populated areas, where efficient transport networks can facilitate the movement of goods and people, stimulate trade, and drive economic growth.

These findings underscore the economic case for investing in road infrastructure. They provide empirical evidence that such investments can boost economic performance, supporting the arguments we've made in this chapter. As Zambia continues to urbanize and develop, the potential economic benefits of improving its road network could be substantial.

In conclusion, road infrastructure is a key driver of GDP, contributing to economic productivity in a multitude of ways. By facilitating the movement of goods and services, reducing transportation costs, and enhancing access to markets, it can significantly boost a country's economic performance. In the following sections, we will explore how these principles apply to the Zambian context, examining the current impact of road infrastructure on Zambia's GDP and the potential benefits of improving it.

Local Perspectives:

The following are responses by locals directly affected by the current state of the roads infrastructure in Zambia, to the question of how better infrastructure can enhance their lives/business.

Joseph Mwenda – a local businessman.

Easy movement of goods. I take things to the border for sale, now because of how bad the roads are, it takes a long time to get there. Also for the fresh products they get spoiled before reaching the border because of spending too much time on the road.

Banda – Premium (Executive) Taxi driver

Bad roads destroy cars, so better roads can increase the lifespan of a vehicle. You constantly have breakdowns because of how bad the roads are.

Miriam Chulu – Concerned Citizen

Good roads will lessen the number of accidents.
When the road is bad, a driver can easily lose
control and have an accident so good roads are
needed to reduce accidents. The road to copperbelt has claimed a lot of lives because of how bad
it is.

4.2 The Direct Contribution to GDP

Investment in road infrastructure has a direct and immediate impact on a country's GDP through the construction activity it generates. This impact is multifaceted, encompassing a broad spectrum of activities and industries that are involved in the process of building and maintaining roads.

Construction Activity

The most immediate contribution to GDP comes from the construction activity itself. Building roads is a labor-intensive process, requiring a large workforce of construction workers, engineers, surveyors, and other professionals. This creates jobs, both temporary and permanent, contributing to employment and income generation. The wages earned by these workers are spent in the economy, stimulating demand for goods and services and further boosting GDP.

Construction Activity

Production of Construction Materials

Road construction also drives demand for a wide range of construction materials, including asphalt, concrete, steel, and aggregates. This stimulates activity in industries such as mining, manufacturing, and quarrying, which produce these materials. It also supports industries involved in the transport, storage, and distribution of construction materials. The increased activity in these industries contributes to GDP and can create additional jobs.

Provision of Engineering and Other Services

Building roads requires a range of services, from engineering design and project management to environmental impact assessment and quality control. The provision of these services contributes to GDP and supports the growth of professional services sectors. It also contributes to the development of human capital, as it requires skilled professionals and provides opportunities for training and skill development.

Maintenance and Repair

Once roads are built, they need to be maintained and occasionally repaired. This ongoing maintenance activity contributes to GDP and provides a steady source of employment. It also supports industries involved in the production and supply of maintenance materials and equipment.

In conclusion, investment in road infrastructure directly contributes to GDP through the construction activity it generates and the ripple effects this has on other sectors of the economy. This direct impact is an important part of the economic case for investing in road infrastructure. However, it is not the only benefit. In the following sections, we will explore the indirect impacts of road infrastructure on GDP, including its effects on trade, productivity, and investment.

4.3 The Indirect Influence on GDP

Beyond its direct contributions to GDP through construction and maintenance activities, road infrastructure also exerts significant indirect effects on a country's economic output. By enhancing connectivity, reducing transportation costs, and minimizing travel times, it can increase the efficiency and competitiveness of various sectors of the economy, leading to a more productive and dynamic economic landscape.

Agricultural Productivity

One of the sectors that can benefit the most from improved road networks is agriculture. In many countries, including Zambia, agriculture is a major part of the economy and a significant source of employment. However, agricultural productivity can be hampered by poor road infrastructure, which makes it difficult for farmers to get their products to market. For instance, a farmer in Ndola who needs to transport his produce to Lusaka would have to endure a nearly 5-hour journey due to the current state of the road network. With improved road networks, this journey could be significantly reduced, allowing the farmer to transport his produce more quickly and cheaply, reducing post-harvest losses and lowering costs. This can boost agricultural productivity and incomes, leading to increased economic activity and higher GDP.

Industrial Efficiency

Improved road infrastructure can also enhance the efficiency of the industrial sector. By reducing transportation costs and times, it can lower the cost of raw materials and make supply chains more reliable. This can increase the competitiveness of domestic industries, stimulate investment, and boost output. It can also attract foreign direct investment, as many multinational companies consider infrastructure quality when choosing where to invest.

Service Sector Growth

The service sector can also benefit from improved road infrastructure. Services such as retail, logistics, tourism, and professional services rely heavily on road transport. Better roads can enhance the efficiency and quality of these services, leading to growth in these sectors. For instance, improved roads can boost tourism by making tourist sites more accessible, leading to increased visitor numbers and tourism revenues.

Social Benefits

Finally, improved road infrastructure can have indirect economic benefits through its social impacts. By enhancing access to markets, jobs, and services, roads can improve living standards, reduce poverty, and enhance social inclusion. These social benefits can translate into economic benefits, as healthier, better-educated, and more connected populations are more productive and can contribute more to GDP.

Potential for job creation and enhanced economic activity

In conclusion, the indirect impacts of road infrastructure on GDP can be substantial, affecting a wide range of sectors and contributing to both economic and social development. These impacts underscore the importance of investing in road infrastructure, not just for its direct economic benefits, but also for its broader contributions to economic productivity and social well-being. In the following sections, we will explore these impacts in more detail, examining how improved road infrastructure could boost Zambia's GDP and contribute to its development goals.

4.4 Amplifying the Impact of Road Infrastructure on GDP with AI and ML

As we delve into the profound influence of road infrastructure on a nation's GDP, it's crucial to acknowledge the transformative role that emerging technologies, particularly Artificial Intelligence (AI) and Machine Learning (ML), can play in augmenting this impact. These technologies have the potential to fundamentally reshape the management and utilization of road infrastructure, thereby enhancing its contribution to economic productivity.

AI and ML, with their ability to process vast volumes of data, discern patterns, and generate predictive insights, can provide invaluable tools for infrastructure management. For instance, these technologies could be deployed to optimize traffic flow, anticipate maintenance requirements, and enhance road safety. Such applications could lead to a more efficient and effective use of the road network, reducing costs, boosting productivity, and ultimately contributing to GDP growth.

Moreover, AI and ML can revolutionize logistics and supply chain management, which are pivotal for the efficient transportation of goods across the country. By forecasting demand, optimizing routes, and managing inventory, these technologies can minimize costs and maximize efficiency, thereby stimulating trade and contributing to GDP growth.

As we continue to explore the potential impact of road infrastructure on Zambia's GDP, it's essential to consider the transformative potential of AI and ML technologies. They hold the promise of not just enhancing the existing infrastructure but redefining how it's managed and utilized. In the final chapter of this book, we will get into how Zambia can leverage these cutting-edge technologies to bolster its road infrastructure and catalyze economic growth.

4.5 Unleashing Zambia's Economic Potential through Road Infrastructure

For Zambia, strategic investment in road infrastructure could catalyze a transformative shift in the economy, stimulating growth across diverse sectors and fostering regional integration. Given Zambia's economic composition and geographical positioning, enhancements to the road network could unlock substantial economic potential and drive GDP growth.

Agriculture and Mining

Agriculture and mining form the bedrock of Zambia's economy, making substantial contributions to its GDP and employment. Both sectors are heavily reliant on efficient transport networks for their operations. In the realm of agriculture, upgraded road networks can enable timely and cost-effective transport of produce from farms to markets, mitigating post-harvest losses and augmenting farmers' incomes. This can invigorate agricultural productivity and stimulate rural development. In the mining sector, improved roads can curtail the cost and time required to transport minerals to ports or processing facilities, bolstering the competitiveness of Zambia's mining sector. This can draw investment, create jobs, and amplify export revenues.

Regional Connectivity

Zambia's geographical position, landlocked and bordered by eight countries, presents a unique opportunity. By enhancing its road network, Zambia can bolster its connectivity with neighboring countries, facilitating regional trade and integration. This could position Zambia as a regional transport hub, attracting logistics and transportation companies, and stimulating the growth of related sectors such as warehousing, distribution, and retail. This could draw additional investment, both domestic and foreign, create jobs, and boost GDP.

Infrastructure-Driven Growth

The process of improving road infrastructure itself can stimulate economic growth. The construction activity generated by infrastructure projects can create jobs, stimulate demand for construction materials and services, and boost economic activity. Moreover, the improved infrastructure can attract investment in other sectors, such as manufacturing and tourism, which value good connectivity. This can lead to a cycle of infrastructure-driven growth, where infrastructure investment stimulates economic activity, which in turn generates revenues that can be reinvested in further infrastructure development.

4.6 Zambia's Economic Landscape and the Role of Infrastructure Development: A Synopsis

Zambia's economic landscape has demonstrated resilience, with real GDP growth bouncing back to 4.6% in 2021 and 3.0% in 2022, following a contraction of 2.8% in 2020. This recovery was primarily propelled by sectors such as wholesale and retail trade, agriculture, and mining and quarrying. Inflation rates also saw a significant drop from 22.1% in 2021 to 10.1% in 2022, largely due to reduced food price shocks. However, the country continues to grapple with high debt distress, with debt levels exceeding 104% of GDP.

The country's trade balance experienced an upturn in 2021, recording a surplus of 12.1% due to increased export volumes and prices, coupled with subdued imports of consumer goods. International reserves also increased from 2.4 months of import cover in 2021 to 3.6 months in 2022, thanks to the Extended Credit Facility and the Special Drawing Rights allocation from the International Monetary Fund. The performance of the financial sector improved in 2021 and 2022, with the nonperforming loans ratio decreasing from 9.0% in 2021 to 6.1% in 2022 due to business recoveries. However, poverty remains a significant challenge, with over 50% of the population living below the national poverty line.

Looking ahead, Zambia's GDP is projected to grow by 4.0% in 2023 and 4.2% in 2024, underpinned by the continued recovery in mining, services, and manufacturing sectors, higher global copper prices, and market confidence associated with ongoing fiscal consolidation measures. Inflation is expected to decline further to 8.5% in 2023 and 7.1% in 2024. However, the country faces several risks, including higher fuel prices, fluctuating copper prices, and the impact of global events such as Russia's invasion of Ukraine on fertilizer and fuel prices. Climate change also presents significant challenges and opportunities, with the country's overall need for climate finance estimated at $50 billion through 2030.

Economic Indicator	2020	2021	2022	2023 (Projected)	2024 (Projected)
Real GDP Growth	-2.8%	4.6%	3.0%	4.0%	4.2%
Inflation Rate	N/A	22.1%	10.1%	8.5%	7.1%
Debt Levels	N/A	N/A	104%	N/A	N/A
Trade Balance	N/A	12.1%	N/A	N/A	N/A
Import Cover	N/A	2.4 months	3.6 months	N/A	N/A
Nonperforming Loans Ratio	N/A	9.0%	6.1%	N/A	N/A

Key Economic Indicators and Projections for Zambia.

Please note that "N/A" is used where the data was not provided or is not applicable

Given this economic outlook, it's evident that Zambia is on a trajectory of recovery and growth. The GDP growth, reduction in inflation, and the projected growth in sectors like mining, services, and manufacturing all point towards a positive economic trajectory.

However, the country's high debt distress and the persistent fiscal deficit are areas of concern. Infrastructure development, particularly in road infrastructure, can play a significant role in addressing these challenges and accelerating economic growth.

Strategic advancements in roads and infrastructure can stimulate economic activity, foster regional integration, and improve the lives of citizens. Improved road infrastructure can enhance access to markets for businesses, particularly in sectors like mining and agriculture, which are key drivers of Zambia's economy. This can lead to increased trade, higher export volumes, and economic growth.

Moreover, better road infrastructure can also attract investment in sectors like manufacturing and services, creating jobs, and reducing poverty. The development of secure rest stops and cargo management facilities can boost the logistics sector, further contributing to economic growth.

Given these factors, with robust advancements in roads and infrastructure, Zambia could potentially see its GDP growth rate increase by an additional 1-2% annually. This would be driven by increased economic activity, improved efficiency, and enhanced competitiveness resulting from better infrastructure.

However, it's important to note that this is a rough estimate and the actual impact could vary depending on a range of factors, including the scale and quality of infrastructure development, the response of businesses and investors, and the broader economic and policy environment.

In addition, the development of road infrastructure should be accompanied by measures to ensure sustainability and resilience, particularly in the face of climate change. This includes incorporating climate-smart designs in road construction, promoting the use of renewable energy in infrastructure facilities, and implementing measures to protect and restore natural ecosystems affected by infrastructure development.

Overall, while the road ahead has its challenges, with strategic and sustainable infrastructure development, Zambia can navigate its way towards a prosperous and resilient future.

In conclusion, investment in road infrastructure could have a significant impact on Zambia's GDP. It could boost key sectors such as agriculture and mining, enhance regional connectivity, and stimulate infrastructure-driven growth. However, realizing this potential requires careful planning, adequate financing, and effective implementation. In the following sections, we will explore these issues in more detail, examining how Zambia can leverage its road infrastructure for economic growth and development.

4.6 Case Study: Dangote Cement Zambia - A Testament to the Power of Infrastructure Investment

As we explore the potential impact of road infrastructure on Zambia's GDP, it's instructive to consider real-world examples that illustrate this relationship. One such example is Dangote Cement Zambia, a subsidiary of West Africa's leading cement producer, Dangote Cement.

Dangote Cement Zambia has been a significant player in Zambia's construction market since 2015. Despite the challenges in the Zambian cement industry, the company has remained optimistic about the long-term prospects, particularly following the 2021 Presidential election. Dangote Cement Zambia aims to leverage Zambia as a regional platform for cement supply, serving neighboring countries such as Malawi, Burundi, and Zimbabwe.

The company's operations in Zambia are underpinned by a robust infrastructure network. Its plant, located in Ndola in the country's Copperbelt province, is strategically positioned near a formidable limestone reserve of more than 240 million tonnes. This location enables the company to produce 1.5 million tonnes of cement annually, supplying a premium product at an affordable price to the Zambian market.

The arrival of Dangote Cement Zambia in the market also had a significant impact on the price of cement in the country. The increased competition forced the price of cement to fall to more reasonable levels, demonstrating how infrastructure investment can stimulate market competition and benefit consumers.

Taking advantage of cheaper cost of Cement after Dangote investment into Zambia

Beyond its core business operations, Dangote Cement Zambia is also committed to sustainability and community development. The company is working towards reducing its carbon footprint by using alternative energy sources and has initiated a massive tree plantation project. It aims to replace 15% of its coal consumption by 2021 and plant over 5,000 new trees annually for many years to come.

In terms of community development, Dangote Cement Zambia employs a workforce that is 95% Zambian and has an annual corporate social responsibility plan that includes community road repairs, water projects, supplying fertiliser to farmers, and school building works. The company also responded to the COVID-19 pandemic by helping the local community with sanitisation and providing educational sessions on how to safeguard against the virus.

In conclusion, Dangote Cement Zambia serves as a compelling example of how infrastructure investment can attract value-adding investments, stimulate market competition, and contribute to economic and social development. As Zambia continues to invest in its road infrastructure, it can expect to attract more companies like Dangote Cement, boosting its GDP and fostering sustainable development.

Reflection and Action Plan:

As we conclude this chapter, I invite you to delve deeper into understanding your country's Gross Domestic Product (GDP) and the role infrastructure, particularly road infrastructure, plays in shaping it.

Reflection:

Ponder over the question: How could enhancements in road infrastructure potentially stimulate the economy in your area? Consider factors such as improved accessibility, increased trade, and the potential for attracting new businesses.

Action Plan:

Take the initiative to educate yourself further about your country's GDP and the impact of infrastructure on it. You could do this by researching online, reading relevant books, or engaging in discussions with local economists or community leaders. Consider how improved road infrastructure could boost economic activity in your area and think about how you can contribute to or advocate for such improvements. Remember, every step towards better infrastructure is a step towards economic prosperity.

5

The Role of Road Infrastructure in Regional Integration

"Good roads, canals, and navigable rivers, by diminishing the expense of carriage, put the remote parts of the country more nearly upon a level with those in the neighborhood of the town. They are upon that account the greatest of all improvements." - Adam Smith.

In this chapter, we delve into the crucial role that road infrastructure plays in fostering regional integration, with a specific focus on Zambia's strategic location within Southern Africa. Regional integration, defined as the process by which neighboring countries collaborate more closely through shared institutions and regulations, is widely acknowledged as a potent catalyst for economic development. Road infrastructure, as an enabler of movement and connectivity, is a fundamental element in this process.

Zambia, a landlocked nation bordered by eight countries, occupies a unique position within the Southern African region. If well-developed and maintained, its road network could serve as a vital conduit connecting several countries in the region. This could not only enhance

Zambia's own economic prospects but also contribute to broader regional integration and cooperation.

We initiate this exploration by providing an overview of the concept of regional integration, discussing its advantages and challenges, and emphasizing the role of infrastructure in this process. We will draw on global examples, including the European Union, the Association of Southeast Asian Nations (ASEAN), and the East African Community (EAC), to illustrate these concepts.

Next, we shift our focus to the Southern African context. We will discuss the current state of regional integration in Southern Africa, the role of the Southern African Development Community (SADC), and the specific challenges and opportunities that this region presents. We will also highlight the significance of road infrastructure in facilitating regional trade, reducing transportation costs, and promoting economic cooperation.

We then concentrate on Zambia, examining its current road network, its strategic positioning, and the potential benefits of leveraging this position for regional integration. We will discuss how improved road infrastructure could enhance Zambia's connectivity with its neighbors, facilitate cross-border trade, and position the country as a regional transport hub.

Finally, we will discuss the policy implications of our findings. We will consider how Zambia can leverage its road infrastructure for regional integration, discussing issues such as infrastructure investment, border management, and regional cooperation. We will also consider how to balance the benefits of regional integration with national development priorities, ensuring that the process of integration contributes to sustainable and inclusive growth.

Through this exploration, we aim to provide a comprehensive understanding of the role of road infrastructure in regional integration and the potential benefits for Zambia. By highlighting the strategic importance of Zambia's position and the potential impact of improved road infrastructure, we hope to provide valuable insights to guide policy decisions and infrastructure investments.

5.1 Unpacking Regional Integration

Regional integration is a strategic process that unifies policies, rules, and regulations among neighboring nations, aiming to stimulate economic cooperation and mutual growth. This approach can catalyze increased trade, investment, and economic expansion, fostering a sense of community among member nations and potentially mitigating regional disparities.

Trade Expansion

A primary advantage of regional integration is the facilitation of trade among member nations. By aligning trade policies, reducing tariffs, and eliminating non-tariff barriers, regional integration can foster the free movement of goods and services across borders. This can result in increased trade volumes, broader market access for businesses, and a more diverse range of goods and services for consumers.

Investment and Economic Expansion

Regional integration can also stimulate investment and economic growth. By creating larger, unified markets, it can attract investment from both within and outside the region. This can lead to increased economic activity, job creation, and income growth. Moreover, by promoting policy coordination and cooperation, regional integration can enhance economic stability and resilience, making the region more attractive to investors.

The Role of Road Infrastructure

Road infrastructure plays a pivotal role in facilitating regional integration. Roads are the physical links that connect countries, enabling the movement of goods, services, and people across borders. A well-developed and well-maintained road network can reduce transportation costs, improve logistics efficiency, and enhance connectivity. This can facilitate trade, promote tourism, and foster people-to-people exchanges, all of which are key aspects of regional integration.

However, for road infrastructure to effectively support regional integration, it needs to be complemented by other measures. These include harmonized transport policies, efficient border procedures, and coordinated infrastructure planning. It also requires investment in related infrastructure, such as border facilities, logistics hubs, and intermodal transport networks.

In the context of Zambia, its strategic location in Southern Africa provides it with the potential to play a central role in regional integration. By investing in its road network and adopting supportive policies, Zambia could enhance its connectivity with neighboring countries, facilitate cross-border trade, and position itself as a regional transport hub. In the following sections, we will look more into these opportunities, examining the potential benefits and challenges of regional integration for Zambia.

5.1.1 Understanding Regional Integration (Continued)

To further comprehend the concept of regional integration and its potential benefits, examining real-world examples can be insightful. The European Union (EU), the Association of Southeast Asian Nations (ASEAN), and the East African Community (EAC) each offer valuable perspectives on the process of regional integration and the integral role of infrastructure.

The European Union (EU), one of the most prominent examples of regional integration, was established in the aftermath of World War II to foster peace and economic cooperation. Over time, it has evolved into a political and economic union comprising 27 member states. A cornerstone of this integration process has been the development of an extensive transport network, including roads, railways, and ports. This network has facilitated the free movement of goods, services, and people across member states, significantly enhancing trade and economic growth within the EU. Moreover, it has contributed to social cohesion and cultural exchange.

The Association of Southeast Asian Nations (ASEAN), established in 1967, aims to promote economic growth, social progress, and cultural development among its ten member states. Infrastructure development, including road infrastructure, has been a pivotal part of ASEAN's integration strategy. The ASEAN Highway Network, for instance, is a project aimed at improving road connectivity among member states. This initiative facilitates cross-border trade and promotes tourism, thereby contributing to regional integration.

The East African Community (EAC) is a regional intergovernmental organization consisting of six countries in the African Great Lakes region in eastern Africa. The EAC is working towards full political federation of its member states. A key initiative in this process is the development of transport corridors, including the Central Corridor and the Northern Corridor. These corridors aim to enhance road connectivity, reduce transportation costs, and stimulate trade within the region.

These examples underscore the potential benefits of regional integration and the crucial role that road infrastructure plays in this process. They demonstrate how roads can facilitate the movement of goods, services, and people, stimulate economic activity, and foster social and cultural exchange. They also highlight the importance of coordinated infrastructure planning, efficient border procedures, and regional cooperation in maximizing the benefits of integration. Drawing on these examples, we will explore how Zambia can leverage its road infrastructure to promote regional integration and drive economic and social development.

5.2 Regional Integration and Infrastructure Development in Southern Africa

The Southern African Development Community (SADC) has made considerable strides in regional infrastructure development, a critical component of regional integration. Infrastructure in this context encompasses regional transport and communication systems, energy, water and sanitation, and meteorology.

Significant Progress in Infrastructure Development

To date, the SADC region has seen the development of 63 regional infrastructure projects. These projects aim to enhance connectivity, facilitate trade, and promote economic cooperation among member countries. They include initiatives to improve road networks, upgrade ports and airports, expand energy grids, and enhance water and sanitation systems.

The Role of Infrastructure in Economic Diversification

Regional integration, facilitated by robust infrastructure, can play a vital role in diversifying economies. By enhancing connectivity and reducing trade barriers, it can stimulate the growth of various sectors, from manufacturing and services to agriculture and tourism. This can reduce countries' reliance on a few commodities or industries, making their economies more resilient and sustainable.

Delivering Food and Energy Security

Improved infrastructure can also contribute to food and energy security. For instance, better road networks can facilitate the movement of agricultural products, reducing post-harvest losses and ensuring food reaches markets. Similarly, regional power grids can enhance access to electricity, supporting industrialization and improving living standards.

Generating Jobs and Alleviating Poverty

Infrastructure development can generate jobs, both directly through construction activities and indirectly through the economic activity it stimulates. This can contribute to income generation, poverty reduction, and social inclusion.

Potential Growth for All Member Countries

Deepening regional integration within the SADC could raise potential growth for all member countries. By creating larger, integrated markets, it can attract investment, stimulate economic activity, and boost growth.

Effective Transshipment Network

With integration and improvements, SADC's ports could form an effective transshipment network, enhancing the region's connectivity with global markets. This could boost trade, attract logistics companies, and stimulate the growth of related sectors.

Air Transport Dominance

Air transport, dominated by South Africa, is the best in Africa. However, there is potential for other countries in the region to develop their air transport sectors, enhancing regional connectivity and boosting tourism.

Limited Access to Electricity

While electricity infrastructure in southern Africa is well developed, access remains limited, particularly in rural areas. Regional integration could facilitate the expansion of electricity access, supporting economic development and improving living standards.

In conclusion, regional integration and infrastructure development in Southern Africa hold significant potential for economic growth and development. However, realizing this potential requires overcoming challenges such as infrastructure gaps, policy barriers, and financing constraints. It also requires ensuring that the benefits of integration are widely shared, contributing to inclusive and sustainable development. In the following sections, we will explore these issues in more detail, focusing on the role of road infrastructure and the specific context of Zambia.

5.3 Zambia's Geographic Advantage

Zambia's geographic position, nestled as a landlocked country surrounded by eight nations - Tanzania to the northeast, Malawi to the east, Mozambique to the southeast, Zimbabwe to the south, Botswana and Namibia to the southwest, Angola to the west, and the Democratic Republic of the Congo to the north - presents both unique challenges and opportunities. This strategic location, combined with its political stability and relatively developed transport infrastructure, offers Zambia the potential to serve as a regional transportation hub, fostering economic growth and development.

Zambia's central location makes it a critical conduit for goods entering from various neighboring countries. Imports arrive via ports in South Africa, Namibia, Mozambique, and Tanzania, and are then transported by truck through various border points. Key among these are Chirundu and Livingstone on the border with Zimbabwe, Kazungula on the border with Botswana, Nakonde on the border with Tanzania, and Sesheke on the border with Namibia. These border points serve as vital gateways for regional trade, connecting landlocked countries in the region to maritime ports and facilitating the movement of goods across Southern Africa.

Enhancing Zambia's road infrastructure could significantly reduce transit times, lower transportation costs, and improve the reliability of supply chains. This could boost trade, attract investment, and stimulate economic activity, not only in Zambia but also in the wider region. For instance, improved road connectivity could make it easier for businesses in landlocked countries like Botswana and Zimbabwe to access ports in South Africa and Mozambique, boosting their trade and competitiveness.

Moreover, Zambia could potentially follow in the footsteps of Zimbabwe, once known as the "*breadbasket*" of Africa. With the right focus on infrastructure development and a knowledge-based approach to agricultural production, Zambia could leverage its fertile lands and favorable climate to become a major food producer for the region. This would not only boost Zambia's economy but also contribute to food security in Southern Africa.

By enhancing its road infrastructure, Zambia could foster regional integration and position itself as a key transport hub in Southern Africa. This could enhance Zambia's strategic importance in the region, attract additional investment, and create jobs. For instance, Zambia could leverage its central location to develop logistics hubs, such as dry ports and freight terminals, that serve the wider region.

However, realizing this potential will require significant investment in road infrastructure, as well as improvements in border management and regional cooperation. In the following sections, we will explore these issues in more detail, examining the potential benefits and challenges of road infrastructure development in Zambia and discussing how these challenges can be addressed.

5.4 Mapping the Southern African Corridors: The Lifelines of Regional Integration

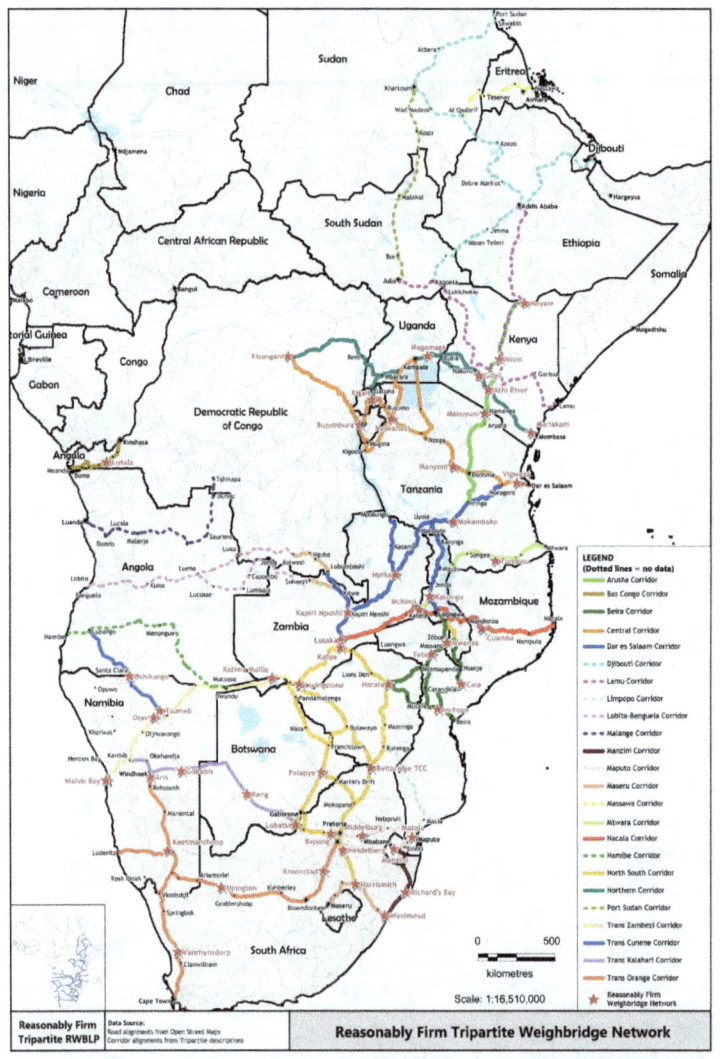

Map showing several major transport corridors cutting through Zambia

Southern Africa is crisscrossed by several major transport corridors that are crucial for regional integration and trade. These corridors, many of which pass through or touch Zambia, are not just roads, but also include railways, ports, and border crossings. They are essential for the movement of goods and people across the region and are a key focus of infrastructure development efforts. Here are a few key corridors:

North-South Corridor:

This is a multimodal and multidimensional infrastructure corridor that links the port of Durban in South Africa to the Copperbelt in Zambia and the Democratic Republic of Congo. It is one of the most important corridors in the region, serving a large hinterland that includes Botswana, Zimbabwe, and Malawi.

Trans-Caprivi Corridor:

This corridor links the port of Walvis Bay in Namibia with Zambia, Zimbabwe, and the Democratic Republic of Congo. It provides a shorter route to the sea for these landlocked countries.

Trans-Kalahari Corridor:

Another corridor that links Walvis Bay with landlocked Botswana and South Africa's industrial heartland, Gauteng. While it doesn't pass through Zambia, it is a crucial part of the regional transport network.

Beira Corridor:

This corridor links the port of Beira in Mozambique with Malawi, Zambia, and Zimbabwe. It is an important route for the export of copper and other minerals.

Nacala Corridor:

This corridor links the port of Nacala in Mozambique with
Malawi and Zambia. It is particularly important for the
transport of coal.

Dar es Salaam Corridor:

This corridor links the port of Dar es Salaam in Tanzania
with Zambia, Rwanda, Burundi, and Uganda. It is a key route
for the export of copper and other minerals.

These corridors can be integrated into the regional integration section of the book by
discussing their role in facilitating trade and economic integration in Southern Africa. They
can also be used to illustrate the importance of road infrastructure and the challenges and
opportunities associated with developing and maintaining these corridors. For example, the
book could discuss how improvements in road infrastructure along these corridors could
reduce transport costs, improve trade competitiveness, and contribute to economic growth
and development in Zambia and the region as a whole.

5.5 The Role of Road Infrastructure in Facilitating Trade

Improved road infrastructure is a linchpin in facilitating trade, serving as the physical conduit that connects producers, consumers, and markets. By reducing transportation costs and travel times, a well-developed road network can significantly boost trade, both domestically and internationally. For a country like Zambia, which is strategically located at the crossroads of several major trade routes in Southern Africa, enhancing its road network could have far-reaching implications for its trade performance and economic development.

Reducing Transportation Costs

Transportation costs are a significant component of trade costs. By improving the quality and efficiency of its road network, Zambia can reduce these costs, making its goods more competitive in regional and global markets. This could lead to an increase in exports, boosting incomes for businesses and farmers. Simultaneously, lower transportation costs can reduce the price of imported goods, benefiting consumers and businesses that rely on imported inputs.

Reducing Travel Times

In addition to reducing costs, improved road infrastructure can also reduce travel times. This is particularly important for perishable goods, which need to reach markets quickly. For instance, the journey from Ndola to Lusaka, which currently takes almost 5 hours, could be significantly reduced with better road infrastructure. This would not only make the journey less frustrating for travelers but also ensure that agricultural products from areas like Ndola reach markets in Lusaka in the best possible condition, maximizing their value and reducing waste. This could boost incomes for farmers and contribute to food security in the region.

Facilitating Cross-Border Trade

Zambia's central location, surrounded by eight countries, means that it plays a crucial role in facilitating cross-border trade in the region. By improving its road network and border infrastructure, Zambia can make it easier for goods to move across its borders. This could increase its exports and imports, boost its role in regional supply chains, and position it as a key trade hub in Southern Africa.

Enhancing Regional Integration

By facilitating trade, improved road infrastructure can also contribute to regional integration. It can help to create a more integrated regional market, where goods, services, and people can move freely across borders. This can lead to increased economic activity, greater competition, and improved living standards. For Zambia, this could open up new markets for its goods and services, attract investment, and create jobs.

Moreover, better road infrastructure can stimulate local economies by attracting businesses and tourists. For instance, major highway systems that bypass small towns could include rest stops and tourist attractions that offer economic incentives for these towns.

In conclusion, improved road infrastructure can play a crucial role in facilitating trade and boosting economic development. For Zambia, investing in its road network could unlock significant economic benefits, enhancing its trade performance, and boosting its role in regional trade. In the following sections, we will explore these issues in more detail, examining the potential impact of road infrastructure on Zambia's GDP, exploring financing options, and discussing how the country can balance infrastructure development with other national priorities.

5.6 The Potential for Zambia to Become a Regional Transport Hub

Zambia's strategic location in the heart of Southern Africa, coupled with the potential for improved road infrastructure, presents a unique opportunity for the country to become a regional transport hub. This could significantly catalyze economic development, attracting additional investment, creating jobs, and stimulating economic growth. However, transforming this potential into reality will require not only substantial investment in road infrastructure but also the implementation of supportive policies and regulations.

Attracting Investment

As a regional transport hub, Zambia could attract additional investment from both domestic and foreign sources. Improved road infrastructure can reduce the cost and risk associated with transporting goods and services, making the country a more attractive destination for businesses. This could lead to increased investment in sectors such as logistics, manufacturing, and retail, which rely heavily on efficient transport networks. Moreover, the development of related infrastructure, such as logistics parks and dry ports, could further attract investment and stimulate economic activity. However, attracting such investment will require a stable and business-friendly environment, including transparent regulations, robust legal frameworks, and efficient public services.

Creating Jobs

The development of Zambia as a regional transport hub could also lead to significant job creation. The construction and maintenance of roads and related infrastructure can generate direct jobs. At the same time, the increased economic activity associated with improved transport connectivity can create indirect jobs in sectors such as logistics, retail, and tourism. This could contribute to income generation and poverty reduction in the country. However, it's important to ensure that these jobs are decent and sustainable, offering fair wages, good working conditions, and opportunities for skill development.

Stimulating Economic Growth

By facilitating the movement of goods and people, improved road infrastructure can stimulate economic growth. It can enhance the efficiency of various sectors of the economy, from agriculture and mining to manufacturing and services. This can lead to increased productivity, higher incomes, and improved living standards. Moreover, by enhancing Zambia's connectivity with its neighbors, improved road infrastructure could position the country as a key player in regional supply chains, further boosting its economic growth. However, this will require supportive policies and measures to enhance the competitiveness of Zambian businesses, such as access to finance, business development services, and market information.

Realizing this potential will require significant investment in road infrastructure. This includes not only the construction of new roads but also the maintenance and upgrading of existing ones. It will also require supportive policies and regulations, such as efficient customs procedures, transparent and accountable governance, and measures to ensure that the benefits of infrastructure development are widely shared.

Furthermore, it's important to consider the environmental and social impacts of road infrastructure development. This includes the potential impact on local communities, natural habitats, and climate change. With careful planning and management, these impacts can be minimized, ensuring that road infrastructure development contributes to sustainable and inclusive growth. This could involve measures such as environmental impact assessments, community consultation, and the use of green technologies in road construction.

In the following sections, we will look more into these issues, exploring the potential benefits and challenges of road infrastructure development in Zambia, discussing potential financing mechanisms, and considering how Zambia can balance the need for road development with other national priorities.

5.6 Case Studies of Successful Regional Integration

To better comprehend the potential benefits of regional integration and the role of road infrastructure in this process, it's beneficial to examine case studies from around the world. These examples offer valuable insights for Zambia as it aims to enhance its regional role and utilize its road infrastructure for economic development.

China's Belt and Road Initiative (BRI)

The BRI is one of the most ambitious infrastructure projects in recent history. This grand plan by China aims to expand economic cooperation and infrastructure connectivity across continents through strategic land and maritime routes. The initiative involves constructing a vast network of roads, railways, ports, and other infrastructure, with the goal of boosting trade, stimulating economic growth, and fostering closer ties among participating countries. According to a World Bank study, the BRI could potentially boost global GDP by as much as $7.1 trillion by 2040 and reduce global trade costs by up to 2.2 percent. This example illustrates the transformative potential of infrastructure development and regional integration, while also emphasizing the importance of meticulous planning, coordination among various stakeholders, and consideration of social and environmental impacts.

European Union (EU)

The EU stands as a prime example of successful regional integration, with its comprehensive transport network playing a pivotal role in facilitating the free movement of goods, services, and people across member states. The Trans-European Transport Network (TEN-T) is a planned network of road, rail, air, and water transport routes in Europe, designed to close gaps, remove bottlenecks, and streamline cross-border transport operations for passengers and businesses. This initiative has not only boosted trade and economic growth within the EU but has also contributed to social cohesion and cultural exchange.

Association of Southeast Asian Nations (ASEAN)

The Master Plan on ASEAN Connectivity 2025 is ASEAN's strategic approach to achieving a seamlessly and comprehensively connected and integrated region that promotes competitiveness, inclusiveness, and a greater sense of community. One of its five strategic areas is sustainable infrastructure. The plan aims to establish multimodal transport infrastructure with smooth and seamless connectivity, facilitating the movement of goods and people across borders.

These case studies underscore the potential benefits of regional integration and the crucial role of road infrastructure in this process. They demonstrate how roads can facilitate the movement of goods, services, and people, boost economic activity, and foster social and cultural exchange. They also highlight the importance of coordinated infrastructure planning, efficient border procedures, and regional cooperation in maximizing the benefits of integration.

In the following chapters, we will explore potential financing mechanisms for road infrastructure, consider how to balance the need for road development with other national priorities, and propose a roadmap for Zambia's future as a regional transport hub.

Reflection and Action Plan:

As we draw this chapter to a close, I encourage you to explore the ways in which road infrastructure has been a catalyst for regional integration in different parts of the globe.

Reflection:

Contemplate the question: How could advancements in road connectivity foster regional integration and cooperation in your region? Consider the potential for increased trade, cultural exchange, and mutual support among neighboring regions.

Action Plan:

Embark on a research journey to understand how road infrastructure has played a role in regional integration elsewhere in the world. You could do this by reading case studies, watching documentaries, or even reaching out to experts in the field. Apply the insights you gain to your own region and think about how improved road connectivity could enhance regional integration and cooperation. Remember, roads are not just about getting from point A to point B; they are about connecting people, cultures, and economies.

6

FINANCING ROAD INFRASTRUCTURE

"The road to success and the road to failure are almost exactly the same." - Colin R. Davis.

I n this chapter, we delve into the complex realm of financing road infrastructure, with a particular focus on the options that could be viable for a country like Zambia. The development of infrastructure, especially road infrastructure, necessitates substantial financial resources. However, the economic and social returns on these investments can be substantial, making them a worthwhile pursuit.

Photo by Josh Sorenson: https://www.pexels.com/photo/brown-concrete-bridge-above-body-of
-water-under-blue-sky-and-white-clouds-103596/

We begin our exploration by examining traditional financing mechanisms, such as government funding and international aid. Government funding, often sourced from tax revenues, has traditionally been the cornerstone of infrastructure development in many countries. On the other hand, international aid has played a pivotal role in infrastructure development in numerous developing countries, with funds often originating from multilateral institutions like the World Bank or bilateral aid agencies.

Next, we venture into more innovative financing mechanisms, such as public-private partnerships (PPPs), infrastructure bonds, and blended finance. PPPs involve a co-operative arrangement between the government and private sector entities to finance, construct, and operate infrastructure projects. Infrastructure bonds are debt securities issued by governments or corporations specifically to fund infrastructure projects. Blended finance, meanwhile, involves the amalgamation of public and private funds to finance infrastructure projects, with the public funds often used to mitigate risk and attract private investment.

We also discuss the role of regional development banks, such as the African Development Bank, in financing infrastructure projects. These institutions can provide loans, grants, and technical assistance for infrastructure development, serving as crucial pillars of support for countries seeking to enhance their infrastructure.

Lastly, we examine the potential role of China's Belt and Road Initiative (BRI) in financing road infrastructure in Zambia. As one of the most ambitious infrastructure initiatives in recent history, the BRI could provide significant resources for road development in participating countries, offering a unique avenue for infrastructure financing.

Throughout this chapter, we will weigh the benefits and challenges associated with each financing mechanism, and how they could be applied in the Zambian context. We will also underscore the importance of fiscal prudence and effective project management in ensuring that infrastructure investments yield the desired economic and social benefits. This includes the need for transparent procurement processes, rigorous project appraisal, and robust monitoring and evaluation systems to ensure that projects are delivered on time, within budget, and achieve their intended impact.

6.1 The Imperative for Sustainable Financing

Investing in road infrastructure is a capital-intensive venture that necessitates substantial financial resources. However, it's paramount that the financing for these projects is sustainable. This implies that the funding mechanisms employed should not only be capable of providing the necessary resources but also be structured in a way that safeguards long-term financial stability.

An over-reliance on debt, for instance, could precipitate financial instability. While loans can furnish the large sums of money required for infrastructure projects, they also necessitate repayment, often with interest. If the debt levels escalate excessively, or if the returns on the infrastructure investments fail to materialize as anticipated, this could lead to financial difficulties. This has been a concern for some countries involved in China's Belt and Road Initiative (BRI), where the large-scale infrastructure investments have been accompanied by significant borrowing.

Therefore, a diversified portfolio of financing sources is often desirable. This could encompass a blend of government funding, loans from international financial institutions or regional development banks, private sector investment through mechanisms like public-private partnerships (PPPs), and grants from international aid agencies. Each of these sources has its own merits and challenges, and the optimal blend will depend on the specific circumstances of each country and project.

For Zambia, the potential role of China's Belt and Road Initiative (BRI) in financing road infrastructure warrants consideration. As one of the most ambitious infrastructure initiatives in recent history, the BRI could provide significant resources for road development in Zambia. However, it's crucial that any financing from the BRI or other sources is structured in a way that ensures long-term financial sustainability.

In the following sections, we will get into these different financing mechanisms, exploring their potential benefits and challenges in the Zambian context. We will also underscore the importance of effective project management and fiscal prudence in ensuring that infrastructure investments yield the desired economic and social benefits.

6.2 Government Financing

Government financing, typically through budget allocations, has traditionally been a primary source of funding for road infrastructure. This method of financing is often perceived as a direct reflection of a government's commitment to infrastructure development, as it involves allocating taxpayer funds to these projects. However, securing adequate government funds for road development and maintenance can be a challenging task, given the myriad of competing demands on government budgets.

Government budgets are finite and need to cover a wide range of public services, from education and healthcare to defense and social welfare. In many cases, these sectors also require significant investment, creating a situation where the needs often outstrip the available resources. This is particularly true in developing countries like Zambia, where resources are limited and the needs are substantial.

Moreover, the allocation of government funds to infrastructure projects is often influenced by political considerations. Infrastructure projects are long-term investments that may not yield visible results immediately. This can make them less attractive for politicians who are focused on short-term electoral cycles. As a result, road development and maintenance can sometimes be overlooked in favor of more immediate, vote-winning initiatives.

Despite these challenges, government financing remains a crucial component of infrastructure funding. It's often used to fund the initial stages of infrastructure projects, such as feasibility studies and preliminary design work. It can also be used to leverage additional financing from private sector investors, who may be more willing to invest if they see a government commitment to the project.

In the context of Zambia, government financing could play a key role in initiating the necessary investments in road infrastructure. However, it will be crucial to ensure that these investments are sustainable and do not lead to excessive debt. Given Zambia's current debt situation, with total external debt estimated at $18.6 billion at the end of 2022, careful financial management, transparency, and accountability in the use of public funds will be essential.

In the following sections, we will explore other sources of financing, such as Road Funds, private sector investment, and international aid, and discuss how they can complement government financing to meet Zambia's infrastructure needs.

6.3 Dedicated Road Funds

Dedicated road funds represent a specialized financing mechanism specifically aimed at road maintenance and development. These funds are often financed by user charges such as fuel levies, vehicle registration fees, or tolls. The principle behind road funds is that those who use the roads and thus contribute to their wear and tear should bear some of the costs of maintaining them. This approach can provide a stable and predictable source of funding for road maintenance, which is crucial for the long-term sustainability of road infrastructure.

However, the effectiveness of road funds largely hinges on their governance and management. Good governance ensures that the funds are used efficiently and for their intended purpose. This includes transparent decision-making processes, clear accountability mechanisms, and regular audits. Without good governance, there is a risk that the funds could be misused or diverted to other purposes.

The management of road funds also plays a crucial role in their effectiveness. This includes the collection of user charges, the allocation of funds to different projects, and the monitoring of project implementation. Effective management ensures that the funds are used in a way that maximizes their impact on road maintenance and development.

In Zambia, the National Road Fund Agency (NRFA) serves as an umbrella fund that holds all road levies, licensing fees, fuel levies, loans, grants, donations, and monies appropriated by Parliament for the roads. This dedicated road fund could provide a sustainable source of funding for road maintenance and development, helping to address some of the challenges associated with public financing, such as the competing demands on government budgets.

However, it is crucial to ensure that the NRFA is governed and managed effectively. This could involve setting up clear rules for the allocation of funds, implementing robust accountability mechanisms, and ensuring transparency in decision-making processes.

In the following sections, we will explore other financing mechanisms, such as public-private partnerships and international aid, and discuss how they can complement dedicated road funds in financing Zambia's road infrastructure needs.

6.4 Private Financing and Public-Private Partnerships (PPPs)

Private financing, particularly through Public-Private Partnerships (PPPs), can be an effective way to mobilize additional resources for road infrastructure. PPPs represent a cooperative arrangement between public and private entities. In the context of road infrastructure, a private entity or consortium typically finances, builds, and operates a road, and recoups its investment through tolls or payments from the government over a specified period.

PPPs can bring several benefits. They can mobilize private capital for public infrastructure projects, potentially allowing for more investment than would be possible through public financing alone. They can also leverage the efficiency, innovation, and technical expertise of the private sector, potentially leading to better quality infrastructure and service delivery. Furthermore, by transferring some of the risks associated with infrastructure projects to the private sector, PPPs can reduce the financial burden on the government.

However, PPPs also come with challenges. They require a robust legal and regulatory framework to protect the interests of all parties and ensure transparency and accountability. They also require careful structuring to ensure that the risks and rewards are appropriately shared between the public and private partners. Moreover, PPPs involve complex contractual arrangements and can take a long time to negotiate and implement.

In Zambia, an example of a PPP in action is the upgrade of the Lusaka-Ndola road to a dual carriageway toll road by a Chinese consortium. The project, valued at US$650 million, is expected to lessen the debt burden on Zambia, which has defaulted on foreign loans necessitating negotiations for a debt restructuring deal with its lenders. However, the project's viability has been questioned due to the difficulty in forecasting traffic and cash flows in less-developed markets, which could impact the project's profitability.

Moreover, the presence of reliable express delivery services, such as DHL, Mercury Express Logistics, FedEx, and the Express Mail Service (EMS) offered by the Zambia Postal Service Corporation, underscores the private sector's reliance on and investment in the country's road network. These services, particularly EMS, which has the widest domestic network, could potentially contribute to or benefit from public-private partnerships aimed at improving and expanding Zambia's road infrastructure.

For instance, these companies could enter into PPPs to finance the upgrading or maintenance of key transport routes, with the costs recouped through user fees or government payments. Alternatively, they could benefit from PPPs by using the improved road infrastructure to expand their services, reach more customers, and grow their businesses.

In the following sections, we will explore other financing mechanisms, such as international aid and regional development bank loans, and discuss how they can complement private financing and PPPs in financing Zambia's road infrastructure needs.

6.4.1 The Role of Tech Companies in PPPs

As we explore the potential of Public-Private Partnerships (PPPs) in financing road infrastructure, it's important to consider the unique role that tech companies can play in these partnerships. Tech companies, particularly those operating in the digital and 'fintech' spaces, bring a wealth of technological expertise and innovation to the table, which can be leveraged to improve the efficiency and effectiveness of infrastructure projects.

Tech companies can contribute to infrastructure projects in several ways. For instance, they can use their technological expertise to develop innovative solutions for managing and maintaining road networks. This could include using Artificial Intelligence (AI) and Machine Learning (ML) technologies to optimize traffic flow, predict maintenance needs, and improve road safety. These technologies can enhance the value and impact of the road infrastructure, leading to more efficient use of resources and better outcomes for road users.

Moreover, tech companies can also bring significant financial resources to PPPs. With their high market valuations and access to capital, these companies can contribute to the financing of large-scale infrastructure projects. This can help to alleviate the financial burden on the public sector and ensure the sustainability of these projects.

In Zambia, the tech ecosystem is growing, with several tech companies, including pan-African e-commerce startup Wasoko, subscription video on-demand platform Wi-flix, technology infrastructure company Liquid Intelligent Technologies, crypto exchange VALR, and 'fintech' unicorn Chipper Cash, recently entering the market. This growth is attributed to factors such as high smartphone usage, a pro-business government administration, and a focus on expanding the country's digital economy.

Partnerships with these tech companies could provide a valuable opportunity for Zambia to harness the power of digital technologies in developing its road network. This could not only enhance the quality and efficiency of the infrastructure but also contribute to the country's digital transformation and economic growth. As we get into the financing mechanisms for road infrastructure, the potential role of tech companies in PPPs is an important consideration.

6.5 International Financing

International financing, encompassing funds from multilateral development banks, bilateral donors, or global initiatives, can play a pivotal role in financing road infrastructure projects. These funding sources can provide the substantial investment required for infrastructure development, particularly in developing countries like Zambia where domestic resources may be constrained.

Multilateral development banks, such as the World Bank, the African Development Bank, and the Asian Development Bank, offer loans, grants, and technical assistance for infrastructure projects. These institutions possess extensive expertise in infrastructure development and can provide invaluable support in project planning, implementation, and management.

Bilateral donors, such as the development agencies of various countries, also contribute funding for infrastructure projects. This funding often aligns with specific objectives, such as promoting economic development, alleviating poverty, or fostering regional integration.

Global initiatives, like the Chinese-led Belt and Road Initiative (BRI), present additional opportunities for infrastructure development. The BRI, one of the most ambitious infrastructure initiatives in recent history, aims to enhance economic cooperation and connectivity across continents through strategic land and maritime routes. For countries like Zambia, the BRI could provide significant resources for road development, as well as opportunities for increased trade and investment.

However, while international financing can provide much-needed resources, it's crucial to ensure that these funds are used effectively and that the projects they finance are sustainable. This requires meticulous project planning and management, robust governance structures, and strong accountability mechanisms.

In Zambia's case, international financing could play a key role in funding the necessary investments in road infrastructure. However, it's crucial to ensure that these investments align with the country's development priorities, are financially sustainable, and deliver the desired economic and social benefits.

Zambia's recent agreement with its official creditors, co-chaired by China and France, on a debt treatment that aligns with the objectives of the IMF-supported program is a significant milestone. This agreement, which includes both a baseline and a contingent treatment that would be automatically triggered if Zambia's economic performance and policies improve, paves the way for sustainable economic growth and poverty reduction.

In the following sections, we will discuss how Zambia can balance the need for road development with other national priorities, and propose a roadmap for the future.

6.6 Charting the Path Forward for Zambia

For Zambia, the journey towards establishing a comprehensive and efficient road network involves strategically harnessing a blend of these financing sources. Each financing avenue—public, private, and international—offers unique advantages and challenges, and the optimal combination will hinge on the specific circumstances of each project and the wider economic and fiscal landscape.

Public financing, facilitated through government budget allocations, can serve as a testament to a government's dedication to infrastructure development and can be instrumental in attracting additional financing from other sources. However, given the myriad of competing demands on government budgets, securing adequate public funds for road development and maintenance often presents a formidable challenge.

Private financing, particularly through Public-Private Partnerships (PPPs), can mobilize private capital for public infrastructure projects, potentially facilitating a higher level of investment than would be feasible through public financing alone. However, PPPs necessitate a robust legal and regulatory framework to safeguard the interests of all parties involved and ensure transparency and accountability.

International financing, sourced from multilateral development banks, bilateral donors, or global initiatives like the Belt and Road Initiative, can provide the large-scale investment required for infrastructure development. However, it's crucial to ensure that these funds are utilized effectively and that the projects they finance are sustainable.

Road funds, financed by user charges such as fuel levies or tolls, can provide a stable and predictable source of funding for road maintenance. However, their effectiveness hinges on the governance and management of the funds.

In harnessing these diverse sources of financing, Zambia could leverage its strategic geographic position to attract investment. As a landlocked country surrounded by eight nations, Zambia has the potential to serve as a regional transportation hub, fostering economic growth and development. This strategic position could render the country an attractive destination for both private and international investment in road infrastructure.

In the forthcoming chapters, we will look further into how Zambia can balance the need for road development with other national priorities, such as education, healthcare, and environmental sustainability. We will also propose a roadmap for the future, outlining the steps that Zambia can take to develop its road network, stimulate its economy, and enhance the lives of its citizens.

Reflection and Action Plan:

As we conclude this chapter, I invite you to delve into the various financing models that exist for infrastructure projects and ponder their potential application in your local context.

Reflection Point:

Reflect on the question: What financing options might be feasible for road infrastructure projects in your community? Consider both traditional and innovative financing methods, and think about how they could be tailored to suit your community's specific needs and circumstances.

Action Plan:

Begin by researching different financing models for infrastructure projects. This could include public-private partnerships, government funding, loans from international financial institutions, or even community crowdfunding initiatives. Evaluate the pros and cons of each model and consider how they could be applied in your community. You might also want to reach out to local government officials or community leaders to discuss these options and their potential feasibility. Remember, the goal is to find a sustainable and effective financing model that can help bring about much-needed improvements in road infrastructure in your community.

7

BALANCING PRIORITIES

"The best way to predict the future is to create it." - Peter Drucker.

I n this chapter, we get into the intricate task of harmonizing the advancement of road infrastructure with other national imperatives in Zambia. While the enhancement of road infrastructure is a pivotal catalyst for economic growth and regional integration, it doesn't stand alone as the sole contributor to a nation's prosperity. A well-rounded approach to national development encompasses a wide array of priorities, including education, healthcare, environmental sustainability, and social equity.

The challenge for policymakers lies in the allocation of resources in a manner that optimizes the collective well-being of the population. This necessitates making tough decisions about where to channel limited resources and how to strike a balance between immediate needs and long-term objectives. It also calls for a comprehensive understanding of the interplay and mutual influence between different sectors. For example, investments in education can bolster the productivity of the workforce, which can, in turn, amplify the economic returns from road infrastructure. Similarly, investments in healthcare can enhance the health and well-being of the population, enabling them to contribute more effectively to, and reap the benefits from, economic development.

In the Zambian context, this balanced approach is of paramount importance. The country grapples with substantial challenges in areas such as education, healthcare, and environmental sustainability. Concurrently, it possesses significant potential for economic growth, particularly through the development of its road infrastructure. Policymakers are tasked with finding the right equilibrium between these diverse priorities, ensuring that the advantages of road infrastructure development are maximized and equitably distributed among the population.

In the subsequent sections, we will look more into these issues, discussing how Zambia can harmonize the need for road development with its other national priorities, and how it can ensure that the benefits of road infrastructure development are equitably distributed. We will also explore the potential social and environmental impacts of road development, and how these can be effectively managed and mitigated.

7.1 Navigating a Multitude of Priorities

Every nation, irrespective of its developmental stage, wrestles with the intricate task of juggling multiple priorities. The art of governance involves making informed decisions about the distribution of limited resources across a diverse range of sectors, each with its unique needs and demands. While the importance of road infrastructure for economic growth and societal well-being is undeniable, other sectors such as education, healthcare, social services, and environmental protection also warrant attention and resources.

Education, for instance, forms the bedrock of any society. It arms individuals with the necessary knowledge and skills to contribute to the economy and to engage fully in social and political life. Investment in education can yield substantial returns in terms of economic growth, social cohesion, and individual well-being.

Healthcare is another pivotal sector. A healthy population is a precondition for economic productivity. Investment in healthcare can enhance the health and longevity of the population, improve the quality of life, and curtail the economic costs associated with illness and disability.

Social services, encompassing areas such as housing, social security, and child protection, play a vital role in supporting the most vulnerable members of society and in promoting social equity. Investment in these areas can alleviate poverty, bolster social stability, and foster a more inclusive and equitable society.

Environmental protection is also a key priority. In the face of global challenges such as climate change, biodiversity loss, and pollution, investment in environmental protection is indispensable for the sustainability of our planet and for the well-being of current and future generations.

In the Zambian context, these challenges are particularly pronounced. The country confronts substantial needs in all these areas, and the task of harmonizing these needs with the need for road infrastructure development is a complex one. It demands meticulous planning, strategic decision-making, and a commitment to sustainable and inclusive development.

In the subsequent sections, we will try to explore more into understanding these challenges in the context of Zambia, and how it can navigate this intricate landscape, striking a balance that optimizes the benefits of road infrastructure development while also addressing its other critical priorities.

7.1.1 Understanding Zambia's Unique Challenges

Zambia, like many developing nations, faces a unique set of challenges that require careful consideration when balancing national priorities. These challenges span across various sectors including education, healthcare, social services, and environmental protection.

In the **Education** sector, Zambia grapples with issues such as lack of resources, poor teacher training, inadequate infrastructure, overcrowding, low progression rates, and challenges with online learning. Despite the importance of education in driving economic growth and social cohesion, only 4% of Grade 2 learners achieved national grade level reading proficiency in the most recent Early Grade Reading Assessment.

Healthcare in Zambia is also fraught with difficulties. The country contends with inadequate infrastructure, a high burden of illness, lack of health resources, poor access to safe water and sanitation, poorly stocked pharmacies, and inequities in access and utilization. The national average poverty rate stands at 54%, and the rural poverty rate at 77%, further exacerbating these healthcare challenges.

Social challenges in Zambia are equally pressing. Economic growth has been poorly shared, with a high national average poverty rate. Children and youth face a myriad of issues, including malnutrition, imprisonment, educational disadvantages, child marriage, hard labor, unemployment, and crime. The country also grapples with human resource constraints and issues with social protection interventions.

Environmental protection in Zambia is a major concern. The country faces high rates of deforestation, water resource management issues, impacts of climate change, pollution from mining, water pollution, and sanitation issues, and low access to clean drinking water. Extreme weather events, particularly in the capital city of Lusaka, pose additional environmental challenges.

These challenges underscore the complexity of the task at hand. As Zambia seeks to develop its road infrastructure, it must also address these pressing issues in education, healthcare, social services, and environmental protection. The following sections will look into how Zambia can strike a balance between these critical priorities.

7.2 Embracing Strategic Planning

Strategic planning serves as a vital instrument in managing diverse priorities and making educated decisions about resource distribution. It necessitates the establishment of distinct objectives, evaluation of available resources, and decision-making based on a thorough understanding of a country's needs and potential.

When it comes to road infrastructure development, strategic planning necessitates a comprehensive evaluation of the existing road network, comprehension of the country's economic and societal goals, and forecasting of future transportation requirements. It also entails an analysis of the potential economic, social, and environmental repercussions of various investment alternatives.

In the Zambian context, a strategic roadmap for road infrastructure could help ensure that road investments harmonize with, rather than detract from, other priorities. For instance, road projects could be strategically designed to bolster the growth of critical economic sectors such as agriculture, mining, and tourism. They could also be planned to minimize environmental impacts and foster social equity, for instance, by enhancing transportation access in underprivileged rural areas.

Strategic planning also encompasses the evaluation of the financial viability of different investment options and the identification of potential funding sources. This includes exploring the potential for public-private partnerships, international financing, and other innovative financing mechanisms.

Moreover, strategic planning is not a static process but a dynamic one. It requires consistent monitoring and evaluation to gauge progress towards objectives, pinpoint any emerging issues or challenges, and make necessary adjustments. This iterative process ensures that the plan remains pertinent and effective in the face of evolving circumstances.

In the subsequent sections, we will delve into how strategic planning can be leveraged in the development of road infrastructure in Zambia, and how it can assist the country in balancing its need for road development with its other national priorities.

7.2.1 Harnessing Emerging Technologies in Strategic Planning

As we explore the role of strategic planning in harmonizing priorities, it's essential to recognize the transformative potential of emerging technologies, particularly Artificial Intelligence (AI) and Machine Learning (ML), in the realm of road infrastructure development.

Strategic planning transcends the mere establishment of clear objectives and resource allocation; it also involves forecasting future trends and leveraging innovative technologies to accomplish these objectives more efficiently. AI and ML technologies, with their capacity to process vast data sets, discern patterns, and make predictive analyses, can significantly augment the planning, execution, and management of road infrastructure projects.

For example, AI algorithms can be employed to optimize traffic flow and predict maintenance requirements, thereby enhancing the efficiency and lifespan of the road network. ML models can scrutinize historical and real-time data to optimize logistics and supply chains, leading to cost reductions and efficiency improvements.

In the Zambian context, strategic planning for road infrastructure should therefore incorporate the potential role of AI and ML technologies. This could involve establishing partnerships with tech companies, investing in data infrastructure, and building local capacity to implement and manage these technologies.

Moreover, AI and ML can also play a crucial role in environmental impact assessments, helping to predict and mitigate the potential environmental consequences of road infrastructure projects. They can also be used to model different scenarios and assess the potential social and economic impacts of different investment options, thereby supporting more informed and evidence-based decision-making.

By integrating AI and ML into its strategic planning, Zambia can ensure that its road infrastructure development is not only balanced with other priorities but also forward-looking and technologically advanced. This approach can help Zambia to build a road network that is not only robust and efficient but also smart and sustainable, capable of adapting to changing needs and circumstances and contributing to a more sustainable and inclusive development trajectory.

7.3 Navigating Social and Environmental Impacts

As Zambia embarks on its journey towards economic development through road infrastructure, it's vital to consider the potential social and environmental impacts that may arise. These impacts can manifest both positively and negatively, and their careful evaluation and management are essential to ensure that road development contributes to sustainable and inclusive growth.

From a social perspective, road construction can lead to the displacement of communities, particularly those in rural or indigenous areas. This displacement can result in the loss of homes, livelihoods, and access to resources, significantly affecting the well-being of these communities. Conversely, improved road infrastructure can bring about substantial social benefits, such as enhanced access to markets, employment opportunities, education, and healthcare services. Therefore, conducting comprehensive social impact assessments and engaging with affected communities is crucial. This engagement helps understand their needs and concerns and develop strategies to mitigate adverse impacts and maximize benefits.

Environmentally, road construction can lead to habitat destruction, biodiversity loss, soil erosion, and pollution. It can also contribute to climate change through the emissions associated with construction and the increased use of motorized transport. However, through meticulous planning and design, these impacts can be minimized. For instance, road projects can be designed to avoid sensitive ecosystems, incorporate measures to reduce soil erosion and pollution, and promote sustainable transport modes.

In the Zambian context, the consideration of social and environmental impacts is particularly crucial. Zambia is home to diverse ecosystems and species, many of which are threatened by habitat loss and climate change. Furthermore, the country grapples with high levels of poverty and inequality, and many communities depend on natural resources for their livelihoods. Therefore, social and environmental impact assessments should be an integral part of road infrastructure projects. Measures should be put in place to mitigate negative impacts and enhance positive ones.

Moreover, the use of advanced technologies such as Geographic Information Systems (GIS) and remote sensing can aid in the planning and design of road projects to minimize environmental impacts. These technologies can provide detailed information about the local environment, helping to identify sensitive areas and design roads that avoid or minimize impacts on these areas.

In the following sections, we will look at how Zambia can integrate social and environmental considerations into its road development plans. We will also explore how the country can balance the need for road infrastructure with its commitments to social equity and environmental sustainability.

7.4 Emphasizing Good Governance

Good governance forms the bedrock of effective, equitable, and sustainable development. It encompasses transparency in decision-making, accountability for resource
utilization, and the active participation of stakeholders in project planning and implementation. These principles are pivotal in striking a balance between various priorities
and ensuring that the fruits of development are equitably distributed.

Transparency in decision-making implies that the processes leading to decisions
are open, clear, and understandable. This includes providing information about the
criteria used for decision-making, the alternatives considered, and the rationale behind
the final decision. Transparency fosters trust, mitigates the risk of corruption, and
ensures that decisions are grounded in evidence and sound reasoning.

Accountability for resource utilization signifies that those entrusted with managing resources are held answerable for their use. This accountability extends to both
financial resources and other assets such as land and natural resources. Mechanisms
to ensure accountability can include financial audits, performance evaluations, and
public scrutiny and feedback systems.

Stakeholder participation in project planning and implementation ensures that
those impacted by decisions have a voice in shaping them. This can encompass local
communities, civil society organizations, private sector entities, and others. Such
participation ensures that decisions cater to the needs and interests of those affected,
leading to more effective and sustainable outcomes.

In the Zambian context, fortifying governance could play a pivotal role in ensuring that road infrastructure development benefits the entire nation. This could involve initiatives such as enhancing the transparency of planning and decision-making
processes for road projects, bolstering accountability mechanisms for the use of road
funds, and involving local communities and other stakeholders in the planning and
implementation of road projects.

Moreover, leveraging digital technologies can further enhance governance. For instance, digital platforms can be used to share information about road projects, gather public feedback, and monitor project progress. This can make the governance process more transparent, inclusive, and efficient.

In the subsequent sections, we will delve into how Zambia can bolster governance in the context of road infrastructure development. We will also explore how this can assist the country in balancing its need for road development with its other national priorities.

7.5 Learning from Global Case Studies: Successful Balancing of Priorities

In this section, we delve into global case studies that exemplify how nations have adeptly balanced the development of road infrastructure with other national priorities. These instances offer valuable lessons for Zambia as it endeavors to enhance its road network while concurrently addressing other critical areas.

South Korea serves as a compelling example. During the 1960s and 70s, South Korea embarked on an extensive infrastructure development program, which included the construction of the Gyeongbu Expressway, the nation's first and most significant expressway. However, the government also acknowledged the importance of investing in education and human capital development. Despite the substantial resources required for infrastructure development, the government sustained high levels of investment in education. This strategy contributed to the creation of a highly skilled workforce, which in turn supported the country's rapid industrialization. Furthermore, South Korea has also made significant strides in digital infrastructure, becoming a global leader in internet connectivity and digital innovation.

Costa Rica provides another insightful example. Despite being a developing country with limited resources, Costa Rica has managed to develop a well-maintained road network that bolsters its thriving tourism industry. Simultaneously, the country has prioritized environmental conservation and social equity. It boasts one of the highest levels of biodiversity globally and has implemented policies to protect its natural resources, including the establishment of national parks and protected areas. Additionally, Costa Rica has a robust social welfare system and high levels of education and healthcare, demonstrating a strong commitment to social equity.

The Netherlands offers a third example. The country boasts a highly developed road network, which underpins its economy and facilitates trade within the European Union. However, the Netherlands has also been a pioneer in promoting sustainable transportation. It has invested heavily in cycling infrastructure and public transportation, and has implemented policies to reduce car usage and promote sustainable modes of transport. The Netherlands' approach underscores the potential for road infrastructure development to coexist with environmental sustainability.

These case studies underscore that balancing the development of road infrastructure with other national priorities is not only feasible but can also lead to more sustainable and inclusive outcomes. They illustrate that through careful planning, strategic investment, and robust governance, countries can develop their road networks in a manner that bolsters economic growth and development, while also addressing social, environmental, and other priorities.

In the next chapter, we will propose a roadmap for Zambia's future, outlining steps that the country could take to develop its road infrastructure in a manner that supports economic growth and development, while also considering other national priorities. This roadmap will draw on the lessons learned from these case studies, as well as the specific context and challenges of Zambia.

Reflection and Action Plan:

As we draw this chapter to a close, I encourage you to contemplate the balancing act between infrastructure development and other national priorities that your country faces.

Reflection Point:

Reflect on the question: How can your country strike a balance between the need for improved road infrastructure and other national priorities? Consider the various aspects that form the backbone of a nation, such as education, healthcare, environmental conservation, and social welfare, and think about how they can coexist harmoniously with infrastructure development.

Action Plan:

Start by identifying the key national priorities in your country. Then, consider how these priorities interact with the need for improved road infrastructure. Are there areas where these priorities align? Are there potential conflicts? How might these conflicts be resolved? You might want to research how other countries have managed to balance these priorities, or even reach out to experts or policymakers for their insights. Remember, the goal is to envision a future where road infrastructure development and other national priorities can mutually support each other, contributing to the overall progress and prosperity of your country.

8

The Road Ahead

"The road to prosperity is not always smooth, but it is the journey that makes us strong. The future belongs to those who prepare for it today." - Adapted from Malcolm X

As we venture into this pivotal chapter, our aim is to sketch a strategic blueprint for Zambia's future, outlining a comprehensive plan for the evolution of its road infrastructure. This roadmap is designed not only to fuel economic growth and development but also to harmonize with Zambia's wider national objectives.

Drawing from the insights gleaned from case studies and principles explored in preceding chapters, we will adapt these lessons to Zambia's unique circumstances. The roadmap will encompass various facets, including the necessity for sustainable financing, the potential of public-private partnerships, the significance of regional collaboration, and the delicate equilibrium between infrastructure development and other national priorities.

We will also explore the potential influence of international initiatives, such as China's Belt and Road Initiative, in bolstering Zambia's infrastructure development. Moreover, we will underscore the critical role of robust governance and strategic planning in ensuring the effective execution of this roadmap.

By the culmination of this chapter, our aim is to present a comprehensive and actionable plan that can steer Zambia's policymakers, stakeholders, and the broader public in their endeavors to enhance the country's road network and, consequently, its economic prospects. This roadmap will act as a strategic guide for transforming Zambia's road infrastructure, setting the country on a trajectory towards heightened prosperity and an improved quality of life for its citizens.

This chapter serves as a precursor to the subsequent chapters where we will review some case studies and explore the future of Zambia in the context of emerging technologies like AI and ML. The roadmap outlined here will provide a foundation for these future discussions, offering a strategic lens through which to view Zambia's potential and the path to its realization.

8.1 Developing a Strategic Plan for Road Infrastructure

A well-structured strategic plan forms the bedrock of any successful infrastructure development initiative. For Zambia, this plan should serve as a comprehensive roadmap, outlining the nation's ambitions for road infrastructure development, pinpointing pivotal projects, and proposing sustainable financing strategies.

The strategic plan should commence by articulating Zambia's objectives clearly. What are the nation's aspirations from its investment in road infrastructure? These could encompass goals such as enhancing connectivity, facilitating trade, stimulating economic growth, and promoting social inclusion. These objectives should be harmonized with Zambia's broader economic and development goals, ensuring that road infrastructure development propels the nation towards its overarching vision for the future.

Subsequently, the plan should spotlight key projects. This could encompass the construction of new roads, the upgrading of existing infrastructure, and the maintenance of the current network. The selection of projects should be grounded in a comprehensive assessment of Zambia's needs and the potential benefits. For instance, priority could be accorded to projects that bolster connectivity in rural areas, enhance cross-border trade, or alleviate congestion in urban areas.

Financing these projects will necessitate sustainable mechanisms. As explored in Chapter 5, this could involve a blend of public financing, private investment, road funds, and international financing. The strategic plan should propose a financing strategy that strikes a balance between the necessity for substantial investment and the imperative of fiscal prudence and debt sustainability.

Moreover, the strategic plan should not neglect the social and environmental implications of road development. It should incorporate measures to mitigate potential adverse effects, such as displacement of communities or environmental degradation. This could involve conducting comprehensive social and environmental impact assessments for each project, engaging with affected communities, and implementing measures to minimize and compensate for any adverse effects.

Furthermore, the strategic plan should consider the transformative potential of emerging technologies like Artificial Intelligence (AI) and Machine Learning (ML). These technologies can significantly enhance the planning, implementation, and management of road infrastructure projects. By integrating AI and ML into its strategic planning, Zambia can ensure that its road infrastructure development is not only balanced with other priorities but also forward-looking and technologically advanced.

Lastly, the strategic plan should incorporate a framework for monitoring and evaluation. This will enable Zambia to track the progress of its road infrastructure projects, assess their impact, and make necessary adjustments along the way. By doing so, Zambia can ensure that its investment in road infrastructure delivers the maximum possible benefits for its economy and its people, propelling the nation towards a prosperous and sustainable future.

The following steps represent this strategy:

1. **Define Objectives:** Start with a clear definition of what Zambia hopes to achieve through its investment in road infrastructure. This could include goals such as improving connectivity, facilitating trade, boosting economic growth, and enhancing social inclusion.

2. **Identify Key Projects:** Based on the defined objectives, identify key road infrastructure projects. This could include the construction of new roads, the upgrading of existing ones, and the maintenance of the current network.

3. **Assess Financing Options**: Evaluate various financing mechanisms, including public financing, private investment, road funds, and international financing. Propose a financing strategy that balances the need for substantial investment with fiscal prudence and debt sustainability.

4. **Consider Social and Environmental Impacts:** Conduct social and environmental impact assessments for each project. Implement measures to mitigate potential negative effects and maximize positive impacts.

5. **Implement Monitoring and Evaluation Framework:** Set up a framework for tracking the progress of road infrastructure projects, assessing their impact, and making necessary adjustments along the way.

8.2 Capitalizing on Zambia's Strategic Location

Zambia's strategic location, nestled among eight nations, presents a unique set of challenges and opportunities. The challenges stem from its landlocked status, which necessitates reliance on neighboring countries for access to ports and global markets. However, the opportunities are rooted in its potential to evolve into a pivotal transportation hub within the Southern African region.

To capitalize on this geographical advantage, Zambia should prioritize the development of key transport corridors that link it with its neighboring countries. These corridors should be optimized to facilitate the swift and efficient transit of goods and people across borders. This could involve enhancing existing roads, constructing new ones, and implementing strategies to minimize delays at border checkpoints. For instance, the establishment of one-stop border posts, where both countries' customs and immigration procedures are conducted, could significantly streamline the border crossing process.

Beyond cross-border corridors, Zambia should also concentrate on improving its internal road infrastructure. This could involve enhancing roads that connect different regions within Zambia, as well as upgrading rural road networks to improve connectivity for isolated communities. By doing so, Zambia can ensure that the movement of goods and people is not only efficient across borders but also within the country itself.

Moreover, Zambia could explore collaborative partnerships with neighboring countries and regional organizations to jointly develop and manage these transport corridors. This could involve sharing construction and maintenance costs, harmonizing regulations and procedures, and jointly promoting these corridors to attract trade and investment.

By capitalizing on its strategic location in this manner, Zambia can transform its road network into a strategic asset that enhances its role in regional trade, attracts investment, and stimulates economic growth. This approach aligns with the broader vision of regional integration, as discussed in Chapter 4, and can assist Zambia in maximizing the benefits of its investment in road infrastructure.

Furthermore, as shown in Chapter 5, Zambia's strategic location places it at the heart of several key trade corridors in Southern Africa, such as the Dar-es-Salaam, Walvis Bay, Beira, and the north-south corridor through Durban, as well as the Nacala Corridor and the routes identified by the Southern African Development Community (SADC) and the Trans-African Highway network. By focusing on these corridors, Zambia can enhance its connectivity with both the subregion and overseas markets, further boosting its potential as a regional transport hub.

8.3 Harnessing Ndola's Strategic Position for Economic Advancement

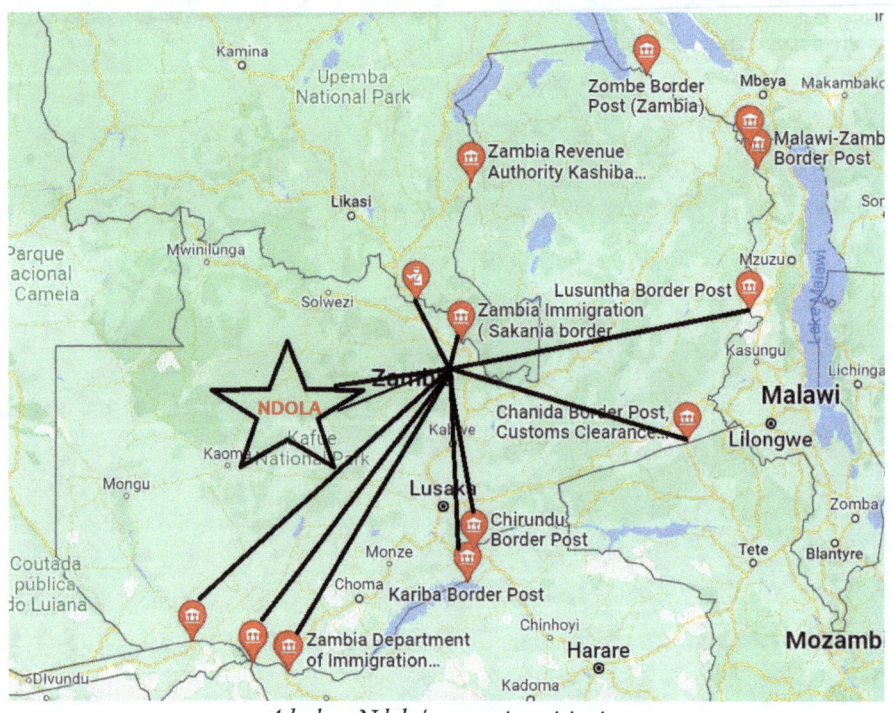

A look at Ndola's strategic positioning

As we've discussed in previous sections, Zambia's geographical location presents unique opportunities for leveraging road infrastructure to stimulate economic development. In this section, we'll look at a specific example of how this can be achieved:

<u>Transforming Ndola into a significant hub for the transit of goods and services</u>

Ndola, situated in Zambia's Copperbelt Province, is strategically located near several border posts, making it an ideal candidate for becoming a pivotal junction in the region's transport network. By implementing a comprehensive road network infrastructure program and positioning Ndola as a central hub, we could potentially redirect a significant portion of cross-border truck traffic through the city.

Projecting the Economic Impact

Let's consider the potential economic impact of this strategy. In 2021, the Chirundu border post cleared 67,542 trucks, which represented about 18.23% of the total traffic volume. If we use this figure to estimate the total truck traffic across all of Zambia's border posts, we arrive at an approximate total of 370,000 trucks per year.

If Ndola becomes a major hub and attracts 25% of this traffic, that equates to around 92,500 trucks per year. The presence of these trucks in Ndola would spur demand for various services, from rest stops and hotels to food services and entertainment. This influx of business could lead to significant job creation and economic growth in the city and its surrounding region.

Moreover, if Ndola could generate revenue comparable to that of the Chirundu border post, which brought in over $4.97 billion in 2021, this could greatly boost the local and national economy.

Wider Economic Advantages

Beyond the direct economic benefits to Ndola and its vicinity, positioning Ndola as a major hub could have far-reaching effects. Improved trade routes could foster increased trade within the region, while better connections between different parts of the country could stimulate national economic activity. The development of Ndola as a central hub could also attract additional investment into Zambia, further contributing to the nation's economic growth.

In conclusion, harnessing Ndola's strategic position by developing it as a major hub for road traffic could bring about substantial economic benefits. While these projections are rough estimates, they provide a sense of the significant potential that such a strategy could hold for Ndola, the Copperbelt Province, and Zambia as a whole.

In this book, we've begun to explore the significant potential that developing Ndola as a major hub for road traffic could hold. However, there is much more to this story - from the detailed planning and investment needed to the broader impacts on society and the environment. We look at these topics in depth in our upcoming book about this strategy. Stay tuned for a comprehensive exploration of how Ndola's transformation into a major hub could shape the future of Zambia's economic landscape.

8.4 Diversifying Financing for Road Infrastructure Development

The financing of road infrastructure is a substantial endeavor that necessitates considerable resources. For Zambia, adopting a diversified approach that taps into various financing sources could be the most effective strategy.

While *government budget allocations* or public financing will undoubtedly form the backbone of infrastructure funding, the competition for these resources is intense. Therefore, Zambia should consider the establishment of dedicated road funds. These funds, sustained by user charges such as fuel levies or tolls, can provide a consistent source of funding for road maintenance and development, thereby reducing the strain on the general budget.

Private financing, particularly through *Public-Private Partnerships (PPPs)*, can also play a pivotal role. In a PPP, a private entity finances, constructs, and operates a road, recouping its investment through tolls or payments from the government. Zambia could explore opportunities for PPPs in road infrastructure, particularly for high-traffic routes or corridors that could generate sufficient revenue.

International financing, from multilateral development banks or bilateral donors, can also provide valuable resources. Zambia should actively engage with these institutions to explore potential funding opportunities. In particular, initiatives like the Chinese-led Belt and Road Initiative could provide significant resources for road development.

Beyond these traditional financing mechanisms, Zambia should also explore innovative options. For instance, green bonds, which are bonds issued to finance projects with environmental benefits, could be used to fund road projects that incorporate green technologies or designs. Infrastructure investment funds, which pool resources from multiple investors to invest in infrastructure projects, could also be a viable option.

By mobilizing a diverse range of financing sources, Zambia can ensure that it has the resources needed to develop its road infrastructure while maintaining fiscal sustainability.

This approach aligns with the discussions in Chapter 5 on financing road infrastructure and can help Zambia maximize the economic and social benefits of its investment in roads.

8.5 Enhancing Governance and Infrastructure Management Practices

The successful implementation of road infrastructure projects hinges on robust governance and effective management. For Zambia, fortifying these areas could significantly boost the efficiency, effectiveness, and sustainability of its road development initiatives.

Transparency forms a fundamental pillar of good governance. It necessitates open communication about the planning, financing, and execution of road projects. This includes disseminating information about the costs, benefits, risks, and social and environmental impacts of projects. By fostering transparency, the Zambian government can cultivate public trust, facilitate informed decision-making, and ensure that road projects align with the country's needs and strategic objectives.

Accountability is another vital element. It involves holding all stakeholders, including government officials, contractors, and financiers, answerable for their actions and decisions. Mechanisms for accountability could encompass regular audits, performance evaluations, and grievance redress mechanisms. By ensuring accountability, Zambia can enhance the quality and sustainability of its road projects, prevent corruption, and ensure that public resources are used effectively and judiciously.

Stakeholder participation is also indispensable. This involves engaging a broad spectrum of stakeholders, including local communities, civil society organizations, private sector entities, and development partners, in the planning and implementation of road projects. Participation can help to ensure that the needs and concerns of all stakeholders are considered, enhance the social acceptability of projects, and foster a sense of ownership and responsibility among the local population.

In addition to these governance principles, Zambia should also strive to enhance the management of its road infrastructure. This could involve adopting best practices in project management, enhancing the technical capacity of the institutions responsible for road development, and implementing effective maintenance strategies to ensure the longevity and durability of the road network.

By strengthening governance and management, Zambia can ensure that its investment in road infrastructure delivers maximum benefits for the country and its people. This aligns with the discussions in Chapter 6 on the importance of good governance in balancing priorities.

8.5 Harmonizing Road Infrastructure Development with Broader National Priorities

The task of harmonizing the expansion of road infrastructure with other national priorities is intricate yet indispensable. For Zambia, this equilibrium is not merely about judicious resource allocation, but also about ensuring that road infrastructure projects are conceptualized and executed in a manner that bolsters broader social, environmental, and economic goals.

From a resource allocation standpoint, it's vital to acknowledge that while road infrastructure is a pivotal catalyst for economic growth, other sectors such as education, healthcare, and social services are equally crucial for the country's holistic development. Consequently, the government should endeavor to distribute resources in a manner that bolsters all these areas. This could involve setting explicit budgetary priorities, exploring innovative financing mechanisms, and capitalizing on international financing where feasible.

From a project design and execution standpoint, road infrastructure projects should be planned and executed in a manner that amplifies their social and environmental benefits. For instance, road projects could be designed to enhance access to essential services in underserved areas, thereby promoting social inclusion and reducing poverty. Similarly, environmental considerations should be integrated into the planning and construction of roads to minimize their ecological impact. This could involve conducting comprehensive environmental impact assessments, using eco-friendly construction materials and techniques, and implementing measures to safeguard local ecosystems.

Moreover, it's crucial to consider the indirect impacts of road infrastructure on other sectors. For instance, improved road networks can boost agricultural productivity by enabling farmers to get their products to market more efficiently and economically. Therefore, investments in road infrastructure should be coordinated with investments in other sectors to maximize their collective impact.

Lastly, as discussed in Chapter 6, strategic planning and good governance are pivotal for harmonizing priorities. By setting clear objectives, involving stakeholders in decision-making, and ensuring transparency and accountability, Zambia can ensure that its road infrastructure development supports its broader development goals.

Developing a robust road network is a challenging but achievable goal for Zambia. With strategic planning, adequate financing, good governance, and a balanced approach to development, the country can transform its road network into a driver of economic growth and prosperity. The journey may be long, but the destination is worth it.

Reflection and Action Plan:

As we draw this chapter to a close, I encourage you to study the realm of public-private partnerships (PPPs) that have been successful in your country or region.

Reflection Point:

Reflect on the question: How could public-private partnerships contribute to road infrastructure development in your community? Consider the unique blend of resources, expertise, and innovation that both public and private sectors can bring to the table.

Action Plan:

Begin by researching successful PPPs in your country or region. Try to understand the key factors that contributed to their success. Was it the alignment of goals between the public and private sectors? Or perhaps the effective risk-sharing mechanisms? Then, think about how these lessons could be applied to road infrastructure development in your community. You might want to engage with local stakeholders, policymakers, or even private companies to discuss the potential for PPPs in your community. Remember, the goal is to leverage the strengths of both the public and private sectors to accelerate the development of road infrastructure, ultimately contributing to the economic and social development of your community.

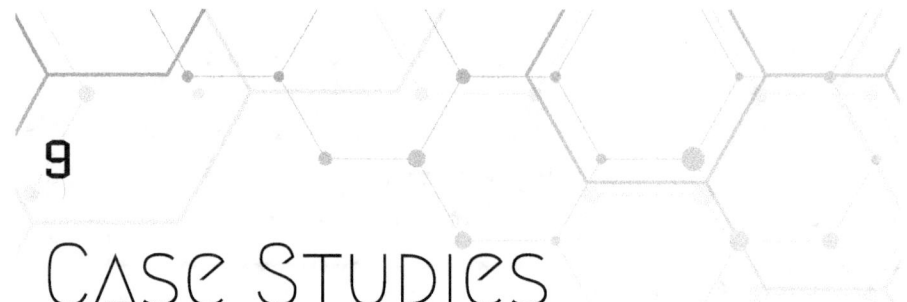

9

Case Studies

"The future is not an inheritance, it is an opportunity and an obligation." - Bill Clinton.

I n this chapter, we embark on a global exploration of compelling case studies that showcase successful strategies in road infrastructure development and financing. Each case study presents a unique narrative of challenges, solutions, and outcomes, offering a diverse array of experiences and lessons learned.

Our objective in presenting these case studies is not merely to highlight the achievements of others, but to distill valuable insights that could be adapted to Zambia's unique circumstances. By examining these cases, we aim to deepen our understanding of effective strategies, potential hurdles, and innovative solutions that can surmount these challenges.

Each case study commences with a brief introduction to the country or region under consideration, outlining the specific road infrastructure challenges they faced. We then look at the intricacies of the strategies they implemented, the financing models they adopted, and the results of their endeavors.

These case studies traverse a wide spectrum of contexts, from the bustling highways of advanced economies to the rural roads of developing nations. Despite their diversity, they all share a common theme - a steadfast commitment to enhancing road infrastructure as a catalyst for economic growth, improved connectivity, and enhanced quality of life for their citizens.

As we navigate through these case studies, we encourage you to contemplate the lessons they impart and consider how these insights could be tailored to Zambia's unique situation. Our aspiration is that these narratives will stimulate innovative thought, ignite engaging discussions, and ultimately contribute to the formulation of robust strategies for road infrastructure development and financing in Zambia.

9.1 Case Study 1:

South Korea - A Leap Towards Modernization

South Korea's journey from a war-torn, agrarian economy in the 1950s to a global economic powerhouse today is a testament to the transformative power of strategic infrastructure development. Central to this transformation was the country's focus on developing a robust and efficient road network.

In the 1960s, South Korea embarked on an ambitious infrastructure development program, with the construction of the Gyeongbu Expressway as its centerpiece. This expressway, which connects the capital city of Seoul to the port city of Busan, was not just the country's first expressway, but also a symbol of its aspirations for modernization and economic growth.

The construction of the Gyeongbu Expressway was a massive undertaking, requiring significant resources and technical expertise. However, the South Korean government recognized that this investment was crucial for the country's economic development. The expressway facilitated the efficient movement of goods and people across the country, supporting the growth of industries and the development of markets.

However, what sets South Korea apart is not just its investment in road infrastructure, but also its simultaneous focus on education and human capital development. Despite the significant resources required for infrastructure development, the government maintained high levels of investment in education. This dual focus on physical and human capital laid the foundation for the country's rapid industrialization and economic growth.

The South Korean case illustrates the importance of strategic planning and prioritization in infrastructure development. It shows that with a clear vision and commitment, even countries with limited resources can develop robust infrastructure that supports economic growth and development.

For Zambia, the South Korean case offers valuable lessons. It underscores the importance of strategic infrastructure investment as a driver of economic growth. It also highlights the need to balance this with investments in human capital to ensure sustainable and inclusive development. As Zambia seeks to enhance its road network, it can draw inspiration from South Korea's strategic and balanced approach to development.

9.2 Case Study 2:

Costa Rica - Balancing Development with Conservation

Costa Rica, a small Central American country known for its rich biodiversity and commitment to environmental conservation, offers a unique perspective on road infrastructure development. Despite being a developing country with limited resources, Costa Rica has managed to balance the need for infrastructure development with environmental conservation and social equity.

Costa Rica's road network, though not as extensive as those in more developed countries, is well-maintained and supports its thriving tourism industry. The country's roads connect its major cities with numerous national parks and protected areas, facilitating access to these natural treasures for both locals and tourists.

However, what truly sets Costa Rica apart is its commitment to sustainable development. The country has made significant efforts to minimize the environmental impact of road construction. For instance, it has implemented stringent regulations to prevent deforestation and protect wildlife during road construction projects. It has also invested in eco-friendly road technologies, such as permeable pavements that reduce runoff and prevent water pollution.

In addition to its environmental efforts, Costa Rica has also prioritized social equity in its infrastructure development. The country has a strong social welfare system and high levels of education and healthcare, ensuring that the benefits of development are shared broadly among its population.

Costa Rica's approach to road infrastructure development offers valuable lessons for Zambia. It demonstrates that it is possible to balance infrastructure development with environmental conservation and social equity. It also underscores the importance of good governance and public participation in planning and implementing infrastructure projects. As Zambia seeks to enhance its road network, it can draw inspiration from Costa Rica's commitment to sustainable and inclusive development.

9.3 Case Study 3:

The Netherlands - Innovation and Sustainability in Transportation

The Netherlands, a small but densely populated country in Western Europe, is renowned for its innovative and sustainable approach to transportation. Despite its size, the country boasts an extensive and efficient road network that supports a highly mobile society and a dynamic economy.

One of the key features of the Dutch approach to road infrastructure is its commitment to multi-modal transportation. The country has invested heavily not only in roads but also in cycling infrastructure and public transportation. This multi-modal approach reduces reliance on private cars, helping to alleviate traffic congestion and reduce carbon emissions.

In addition to its multi-modal approach, the Netherlands has also been a pioneer in the use of innovative technologies in road construction and maintenance. For instance, it has experimented with "smart highways" that use interactive lighting and road markings to improve safety and efficiency. It has also used recycled materials in road construction, reducing the environmental impact of these projects.

Furthermore, the Netherlands has a robust system for financing road infrastructure. The country uses a combination of public funding, user charges, and private investment to finance its road network. This diversified approach ensures a steady stream of funding for road maintenance and development, while also encouraging efficient use of the road network.

The Dutch case offers valuable insights for Zambia. It demonstrates the potential of a multi-modal and innovative approach to road infrastructure. It also underscores the importance of sustainable financing mechanisms and the potential benefits of incorporating environmental considerations into road development. As Zambia seeks to enhance its road network, it can draw inspiration from the Dutch commitment to innovation, sustainability, and efficiency in transportation.

9.5 Case Study 4:

The United States Interstate Highway System: A Case Study in Transformative Infrastructure and Its Implications for Zambia

The United States Interstate Highway System, initiated in the 1950s under President Dwight D. Eisenhower, stands as a testament to the transformative power of strategic infrastructure investment. Spanning approximately 47,000 miles and connecting all 48 contiguous states, this monumental project facilitated interstate commerce, boosted suburban development, and shaped the country's growth patterns.

The economic impact of the Interstate Highway System has been profound. According to a study titled "Infrastructure and Economic Growth: Evidence from the United States," infrastructure spending positively and significantly impacted economic growth. The authors noted that shocks to infrastructure spending had positive and persistent effects on economic growth.

The Interstate Highway System also played a crucial role in facilitating trade and commerce. By providing a reliable and efficient means of transporting goods across the country, the highway system stimulated economic activity and fostered growth. It also facilitated the movement of people, contributing to the growth of suburban communities and shaping the country's demographic patterns.

For Zambia, a landlocked nation strategically positioned in the heart of Southern Africa, the U.S. case offers valuable lessons as the country embarks on its "moon-shot moment." The transformative potential of a well-planned and well-executed highway network is clear. By enhancing its road network, Zambia can stimulate its own economy and carve out a role for itself as a regional transportation nexus, promoting economic integration and collaboration across Southern Africa.

Zambia's key trade routes, including Dar-es-Salaam, Walvis Bay, Beira, and the north-south corridor through Durban, link the country and the Democratic Republic of Congo to overseas markets. These routes are crucial for Zambia's main export partners, which include

Switzerland, China, Singapore, the Democratic Republic of the Congo, and Luxembourg. Enhancing these routes, along with the country's main roads such as the Great North Road, T2 road, T1 road, T3 road, and T4 road, can significantly improve the efficiency of trade and commerce.

The U.S. Interstate Highway System underscores the importance of strategic planning, sustained investment, and a commitment to overcoming challenges. As Zambia seeks to enhance its road network, it can draw on the U.S. experience to guide its efforts. This could involve strategic planning to identify and prioritize the development of key trade routes and main roads, ensuring their maintenance, and exploring various financing options, including public-private partnerships, development aid, and concessional loans.

In conclusion, the U.S. Interstate Highway System offers a compelling case study in the transformative power of infrastructure investment. By learning from the U.S. experience, Zambia can maximize the benefits of its infrastructure projects, stimulate economic growth, facilitate commerce, and shape societal development, achieving its "moon-shot moment."

9.5 Other Case Studies:

In this section, we will briefly explore three additional case studies that offer valuable insights into different aspects of road infrastructure development. These include the United States Highway Network System, which showcases the transformative potential of a well-planned and extensive highway network; the German Autobahn, which exemplifies the importance of quality and efficiency in road infrastructure; and the Trans-African Highway Network, which illustrates the potential of regional cooperation in infrastructure development. Each of these examples provides unique lessons that can inform Zambia's approach to enhancing its road network.

9.5.1 The German Autobahn

Germany's Autobahn is renowned for its high-quality roads and absence of a general speed limit. The Autobahn network, which began in the 1930s, has played a crucial role in Germany's economic development, facilitating efficient transportation of goods and people across the country. The Autobahn is also a testament to Germany's commitment to quality and efficiency in infrastructure development. For Zambia, the German case underscores the importance of quality and efficiency in road infrastructure.

9.5.2 Trans-African Highway Network

The Trans-African Highway Network is an ambitious project to connect Africa from north to south and east to west with high-quality roads. While the project is still underway and faces significant challenges, it illustrates the potential of regional cooperation in infrastructure development. The completed sections have already had a significant impact on trade and mobility in several African countries. For Zambia, the Trans-African Highway Network offers a vision of what enhanced regional connectivity could achieve.

9.5.3 AI in Road Infrastructure Management in Pittsburgh, PA

In Pittsburgh, Pennsylvania, USA, the city has successfully implemented AI in its road infrastructure management. The city uses a system called Surtrac, developed by Carnegie Mellon University, which uses AI to optimize traffic signals in real-time. The system uses machine learning algorithms to predict traffic conditions and adjust signal timings accordingly, reducing waiting times and improving traffic flow.

This case study demonstrates how AI can be used to enhance the efficiency of road infrastructure management. It also highlights the importance of collaboration between cities and academic institutions in driving innovation in infrastructure management.

For Zambia, this case study provides a practical example of how AI can be used to improve road infrastructure management. It suggests that Zambia could explore similar partnerships with universities or tech companies to develop AI solutions tailored to its specific needs.

9.5.4 The Correlation between Transport Infrastructure and Economic Performance in Japan and Selected European Countries

In a comprehensive study conducted by researchers from the University of Antwerp and the University of Tokyo, the relationship between transport infrastructure and economic performance was examined in the context of Japan and selected European countries. The study aimed to understand the impact of transport infrastructure, including road networks, on the economic performance of these countries.

The researchers found a significant positive correlation between transport infrastructure and economic performance. This means that improvements in transport infrastructure were associated with increased economic performance. The strength of this relationship was measured using a correlation coefficient, with values closer to 1 indicating a stronger positive correlation.

Interestingly, the study also revealed that the correlation was particularly strong in countries with a high degree of urbanization. This suggests that the benefits of transport infrastructure investment may be even greater in densely populated areas, where efficient transport networks can facilitate the movement of goods and people, stimulate trade, and drive economic growth.

This case study provides empirical evidence supporting the economic case for investing in road infrastructure. It demonstrates that such investments can boost economic performance, not just in developing countries like Zambia, but also in highly urbanized countries like Japan and those in Europe. As Zambia continues to urbanize and develop, the potential economic benefits of improving its road network could be substantial. This case study serves as a valuable reference for policymakers and stakeholders in Zambia as they consider strategies for road infrastructure development.

9.6 Streamlining Export Procedures: The Role of Customs and Infrastructure

The efficiency of export procedures, particularly customs requirements and border crossing processes, is a critical factor in international trade. For a landlocked country like Zambia, these processes are inextricably linked with the state of the nation's road infrastructure.

In Zambia, as in many countries, exporters must provide a customs declaration form and a commercial invoice for clearance. However, the effectiveness of this process can be significantly impacted by the condition of the country's road network and the efficiency of procedures at border crossings.

At present, Zambian border crossings often experience delays due to congestion and lengthy inspection procedures. These delays extend transit times, inflate transportation costs, and can negatively impact the competitiveness of Zambian goods in international markets. Furthermore, they can lead to spoilage of perishable goods, further eroding the profitability of exporters.

Enhancing Zambia's road infrastructure and refining border processes could substantially improve the country's export efficiency. For instance, upgrading roads leading to border crossings could alleviate congestion and facilitate smoother movement of goods. Similarly, modernizing border facilities and adopting digital technologies could expedite inspection procedures and reduce waiting times.

The Southern African Customs Union (SACU), which includes Botswana, Lesotho, Namibia, South Africa, and Eswatini, offers a relevant case study. SACU has implemented a common customs area, which has streamlined customs procedures and reduced transit times for goods. This has been complemented by infrastructure improvements, particularly the development of major transport corridors.

In Southeast Asia, the ASEAN Single Window initiative has integrated national single windows of member countries into a regional platform, simplifying customs procedures and reducing processing times for cross-border trade. This initiative has been supported by infrastructure development projects, including the ASEAN Highway Network and the Singapore-Kunming Rail Link.

These examples highlight the potential economic benefits of investing in road infrastructure development and streamlining customs procedures. For Zambia, adopting a similar approach could boost its trade competitiveness, attract investment, and stimulate economic growth. This approach would involve a comprehensive review of current customs procedures, an assessment of infrastructure needs, and the development of a strategic plan to address these areas.

8.7 Lessons for Zambia

Drawing from the diverse experiences of countries around the world, Zambia can glean several valuable lessons to guide its approach to road infrastructure development.

Firstly, the importance of dedicated funding mechanisms cannot be overstated. As seen in the case of the United States Highway Trust Fund, dedicated funding sources can provide a reliable stream of revenue for road construction and maintenance. For Zambia, establishing a similar mechanism, perhaps through a road fund financed by user charges or fuel levies, could help ensure sustainable financing for road infrastructure.

Secondly, the potential role of Public-Private Partnerships (PPPs) is worth exploring. As demonstrated by the success of the Autobahn in Germany, PPPs can mobilize additional resources for road infrastructure and bring in private sector efficiency. In Zambia, engaging the private sector, including companies like DHL and FedEx that rely heavily on the road network, could help enhance the quality and coverage of the road network.

Thirdly, the benefits of regional cooperation are clear. The Trans-African Highway Network and the ASEAN Highway Network are testament to the potential of regional cooperation in infrastructure development. For Zambia, enhancing cooperation with its neighbors could help improve cross-border connectivity and position the country as a regional transport hub.

Lastly, the need to balance road infrastructure development with other priorities is a crucial lesson. As seen in the case of China's Belt and Road Initiative, while infrastructure development can stimulate economic growth, it's also essential to consider social and environmental impacts. For Zambia, strategic planning and good governance will be key to ensuring that road development complements, rather than competes with, other national priorities.

In the next chapter, we will build on these lessons to propose a roadmap for the future. This will outline steps that Zambia could take to develop its road infrastructure in a way that supports economic growth and development, while also considering other national priorities.

Reflection and Action Plan:

As we conclude this chapter, let's take a moment to reflect on the power of learning from global success stories in road infrastructure projects.

Reflection Point:

Ponder on the question: What valuable lessons can be gleaned from successful road infrastructure projects in other countries? Think about the strategies, policies, and practices that have led to successful outcomes in these projects.

Action Plan:

Begin by researching successful road infrastructure projects from around the world. Look for common themes and strategies that have led to their success. Consider how these lessons could be applied in your own context. Are there certain strategies that could be adapted to suit your local conditions? Are there innovative solutions that could be implemented in your community? As you review these case studies, take notes and consider how these insights could inform future infrastructure projects in your area. Remember, the goal is not to replicate these projects exactly, but to learn from them and adapt their successful strategies to your own unique context.

10

HARNESSING AI AND MACHINE LEARNING

A New Era for Zambia's Transportation Infrastructure

"Artificial Intelligence, deep learning, machine learning — whatever you're doing if you don't understand it — learn it. Because otherwise you're going to be a dinosaur within 3 years." - Mark Cuban

In this chapter, we review the exciting realm of Artificial Intelligence (AI) and Machine Learning (ML) technologies, focusing on their potential to revolutionize Zambia's transportation landscape and road infrastructure. As we navigate the currents of the Fourth Industrial Revolution, these cutting-edge technologies are transforming sectors globally, and the domain of transportation and infrastructure is ripe for such innovation.

AI and ML present a suite of inventive solutions to the myriad challenges that Zambia's road network currently faces. From predictive maintenance and intelligent traffic management to strategic planning powered by data and the advent of autonomous vehicles, these technologies have the potential to significantly boost the efficiency, safety, and sustainability of Zambia's transportation ecosystem.

We will journey through the various applications of AI and ML in road infrastructure, discussing the potential benefits and challenges, and exploring how Zambia could harness these technologies to optimize its road network. We will also draw lessons from global case studies where AI and ML have been successfully integrated into the transportation sector, offering valuable insights for Zambia.

In the sections that follow, we will explore how AI and ML can enhance strategic planning for road infrastructure, revolutionize the management and maintenance of roads, optimize traffic management, and potentially transform the way goods and people move. We will also delve into the potential role of these technologies in innovating financing mechanisms for road infrastructure and ensuring robust governance.

As we navigate these topics, it's crucial to bear in mind that while AI and ML offer immense potential, their successful deployment requires thoughtful planning, sufficient resources, and a conducive regulatory environment. Therefore, we will also discuss the steps Zambia could take to foster an environment conducive to the adoption and growth of these technologies.

By embracing the power of AI and ML, Zambia has the unique opportunity to leapfrog traditional stages of infrastructure development, ushering in an era of intelligent, sustainable, and efficient transportation. This could significantly propel the country's economic growth and development, positioning Zambia as a pioneer in transportation innovation within the region.

10.1 Harnessing AI and Machine Learning for Efficient Infrastructure Management

Artificial Intelligence (AI) and Machine Learning (ML) are revolutionizing the way we manage infrastructure by providing powerful tools for data analysis, pattern recognition, and predictive modeling. When applied to road networks, these technologies can significantly enhance traffic management, maintenance forecasting, and road safety.

AI and ML can be utilized to optimize traffic flow by analyzing real-time and historical traffic data. This analysis can identify congestion-prone areas, forecast traffic patterns, and suggest optimal traffic management strategies. The result is a potential reduction in travel times, improved fuel efficiency, and decreased emissions, all contributing to a more sustainable and efficient transportation system.

Furthermore, Machine Learning models can leverage data on road conditions, weather patterns, and traffic volumes to predict maintenance needs. This predictive maintenance approach allows for proactive infrastructure management, potentially extending the lifespan of roads, reducing maintenance costs, and minimizing traffic disruptions.

AI and ML also have a significant role to play in enhancing road safety. By analyzing data on accidents, traffic violations, and road conditions, these technologies can identify high-risk areas and suggest interventions to improve safety. For instance, AI could analyze video footage from traffic cameras to detect dangerous driving behaviors, providing valuable insights for law enforcement and traffic management decisions.

In a country like Zambia, where resources for infrastructure management may be constrained, the efficiency gains from AI and ML can be particularly impactful. These technologies can enable more informed and proactive decision-making, helping to optimize resource utilization, maximize the benefits of road infrastructure, and ultimately contribute to economic growth and development.

In the subsequent sections, we will delve deeper into these applications of AI and ML, exploring how they could be implemented in the context of Zambia's road network to drive efficiency and innovation.

10.2 Harnessing AI and ML: The UNCDF Initiative in Zambia

The United Nations Capital Development Fund (UNCDF) has recognized the transformative potential of Artificial Intelligence (AI) and Machine Learning (ML) in Zambia. Through a capacity-building initiative, UNCDF aims to upskill at least 40 individuals working in data-related positions, including selected students in the field of computer science, on data management, AI, and ML.

This initiative is a testament to the growing recognition of the power of AI and ML in driving outcomes around inclusive digital economies and expanding Digital Financial Services for marginalized segments such as women, youth, and other vulnerable groups in low-income brackets. The UNCDF's investment of up to US$ 50,000 into a qualified firm for capacity building is a significant step towards realizing this potential.

The objectives of this initiative are twofold. Firstly, it aims to equip public and private sector partners with the skills to leverage AI, ML, big data, and digital systems to deepen digital economies and financial inclusion. This could involve using AI and ML to analyze traffic data, optimize traffic flow, predict maintenance needs, and improve road safety, thereby enhancing the efficiency and sustainability of Zambia's transportation system.

Secondly, the initiative seeks to help government partners explore policy and regulatory opportunities that advance the application of digital technologies. This could involve developing policies that support the use of AI and ML in road infrastructure management, such as data sharing policies, privacy regulations, and guidelines for the ethical use of AI.

By building capacity in AI and ML, Zambia can equip its workforce with the skills needed to harness these technologies for the benefit of its road network and broader economy. This initiative could serve as a springboard for further investments in AI and ML, paving the way for Zambia to become a leader in the application of these technologies in the region.

10.3 Revolutionizing Logistics and Supply Chains with AI/ML

Artificial Intelligence (AI) and Machine Learning (ML) are not only transforming road infrastructure management but are also revolutionizing logistics and supply chains, which are vital for the efficient movement of goods across Zambia. These advanced technologies can optimize various aspects of logistics, from demand forecasting and route optimization to supply chain visibility and traceability.

10.3.1 Demand Forecasting and Inventory Management

One of the key applications of AI/ML in logistics is demand forecasting. ML algorithms can analyze historical sales data, along with other factors such as economic indicators, weather patterns, and seasonal trends, to predict future demand for different products. This can help companies manage their inventory more effectively, reducing storage costs and minimizing the risk of stockouts or overstocking. In a country like Zambia, where resources are often limited, these efficiency gains could have a significant economic impact.

10.3.2 Route Optimization

AI/ML can also be used to optimize routing for deliveries. By analyzing data on traffic conditions, roadworks, and other factors, AI algorithms can suggest the most efficient routes for trucks. This can reduce fuel consumption and emissions, lower transportation costs, and improve delivery times. In Zambia, where the trucking industry plays a crucial role in the economy, these efficiency gains could have a significant economic impact.

10.3.3 Supply Chain Visibility and Traceability

Furthermore, AI/ML can enhance supply chain visibility and traceability. By integrating data from different stages of the supply chain, these technologies can provide real-time information on the status of goods, from production to delivery. This can improve coordination among supply chain partners, enhance customer service, and enable more proactive management of potential disruptions.

10.3.4 Case Study: Improving Zambia's Health Sector Supply Chain

In the context of Zambia's health sector, the adoption of AI/ML could support the country's economic development by enhancing the efficiency of the transportation sector, reducing costs for businesses, and improving the competitiveness of Zambian products in regional and global markets.

Zambia's health sector faces challenges common in the developing world, such as demand for essential medicines exceeding supply, seasonality affecting demand, and supply challenges due to remote locations and poor weather. AI and ML could be used to optimize the distribution of medicines and medical supplies, predict demand, and improve the responsiveness of the supply chain to local needs and seasonality.

For instance, ML algorithms could analyze historical usage data, population health metrics, and other relevant factors to predict future demand for different medicines and medical supplies. This could enable more accurate and efficient inventory management, reducing the risk of stockouts or overstocking.

Similarly, AI could be used to optimize the routing of deliveries, taking into account factors such as road conditions, traffic patterns, and weather forecasts. This could reduce transportation costs, improve delivery times, and ensure that medicines and medical supplies reach the people who need them most, even in remote and hard-to-reach areas.

By harnessing the power of AI and ML, Zambia's health sector could transform its supply chain, enhancing the availability and accessibility of essential medicines and medical supplies, improving patient outcomes, and contributing to the country's broader health and development goals.

10.4 Navigating the Implementation of AI/ML in Zambia: Challenges and Strategies

While the potential of Artificial Intelligence (AI) and Machine Learning (ML) to revolutionize Zambia's road network and transportation systems is immense, the path to implementation is not without its unique set of challenges. These range from the need for robust data infrastructure and regulatory frameworks to capacity building and managing social and economic impacts.

10.4.1 Building a Robust Data Infrastructure

AI/ML technologies are heavily reliant on data. Therefore, a critical step towards their implementation is the establishment of a robust data infrastructure. This involves the collection, storage, and processing of large volumes of data. For road infrastructure, this could include data on traffic volumes, road conditions, weather patterns, and more. For logistics and supply chains, relevant data could include information on demand, inventory levels, delivery times, and more. Zambia will need to invest in data collection technologies, such as sensors and IoT devices, as well as data storage and processing capabilities.

10.4.2 Developing Comprehensive Regulatory Frameworks

The use of AI/ML technologies raises several regulatory and ethical issues, such as data privacy and security, algorithmic bias, and accountability for AI decisions. Zambia will need to develop comprehensive regulatory frameworks that address these issues, striking a balance between harnessing the benefits of AI/ML and protecting individual rights and societal values.

10.4.3 Investing in Capacity Building

The successful implementation of AI/ML technologies requires a certain level of technical expertise. Zambia will need to invest in education and training to develop local skills and capacity in AI/ML. This could involve partnerships with universities, technical training programs, and collaborations with international tech companies.

10.4.4 Managing Social and Economic Impacts

In addition to these challenges, Zambia will need to consider the potential social and economic impacts of AI/ML. For example, while these technologies can improve efficiency and reduce costs, they could also lead to job displacement in certain sectors. Therefore, it's important to consider strategies for managing these impacts, such as retraining programs and social safety nets.

In the following sections, we will disect these challenges and propose potential strategies for overcoming them, thereby harnessing the transformative power of AI/ML for Zambia's road network and transportation systems.

10.5 Case Study: Harnessing AI/ML to Enhance Supply Chain Data Reporting in Zambia's Serenje District

In this section, we delve into a compelling case study from Zambia's Serenje District, where innovative strategies were employed to improve supply chain data reporting. This case study provides valuable insights into how Artificial Intelligence (AI) and Machine Learning (ML) can be harnessed to enhance data reporting and management in Zambia's road network.

The Serenje District, with its 28 facilities reporting data through Zambia's electronic logistics management information system (LMIS), faced significant challenges in data reporting. In 2018, the average monthly reporting rate was a mere 32 percent, indicating a pressing need for improvement. In response, the district health officers (DHOs) implemented several strategies to enhance reporting:

10.5.1 Positive Reinforcement

The DHOs utilized a WhatsApp group to communicate with all staff responsible for reporting. They sent reminders to conduct physical stock counts, update stock control cards, and prepare logistics reports. They also acknowledged facilities that submitted reports on time or showed improvement, which motivated staff to continue their efforts. AI/ML could be used to automate these reminders and acknowledgments, making the process more efficient and scalable.

10.5.2 Performance Management

The District Health Management Team (DHMT) provided support by ensuring that facility staff were aware they were being monitored. The DHMT also facilitated timely submission of reports by providing transport for the collection of reports from hard-to-reach facilities and sharing data bundles for sending reports via WhatsApp or the electronic LMIS. AI/ML could be used to monitor reporting rates in real-time, identify facilities that are lagging behind, and suggest targeted interventions.

10.5.3 Partner Support

Several partners, including GHSC-PSM, USAID SAFE, and the USAID eSCMIS Project, played essential roles in strengthening supply chain management. They provided support in areas such as monitoring reporting rates, providing supportive supervision, training health workers, and resolving issues related to reporting and LMIS use. AI/ML could be used to enhance these support activities, for instance, by providing personalized training recommendations based on each worker's performance and learning needs.

As a result of these efforts, the district has seen a significant increase in reporting over the past two years, and the availability of essential medicines has improved. This case study underscores the potential of AI/ML to enhance data reporting and management in Zambia's road network, contributing to more efficient and effective infrastructure development.

10.6 Future Directions: Harnessing AI and ML to Revolutionize Zambia's Road Network

As we conclude this chapter, we look towards the future, envisioning a transformative role for Artificial Intelligence (AI) and Machine Learning (ML) in reshaping Zambia's road network. Drawing from the insights gleaned from global initiatives and local case studies, we propose a roadmap for leveraging these advanced technologies to enhance various aspects of Zambia's transportation system.

10.6.1 Traffic Management

AI and ML can be instrumental in optimizing traffic flow across Zambia's road network. By analyzing real-time and historical traffic data, AI algorithms can identify congestion hotspots, predict traffic patterns, and suggest optimal traffic management strategies. This could significantly reduce travel times, improve fuel efficiency, and reduce emissions, contributing to a more sustainable and efficient transportation system.

10.6.2 Predictive Maintenance

AI and ML can revolutionize the way Zambia manages and maintains its road infrastructure. Machine Learning models can use data on road conditions, weather patterns, and traffic volumes to predict where and when maintenance will be needed. This proactive approach to infrastructure management can extend the lifespan of roads, reduce maintenance costs, and minimize disruptions to traffic.

10.6.3 Road Safety

AI and ML can play a pivotal role in enhancing road safety. By analyzing data on accidents, traffic violations, and road conditions, these technologies can identify high-risk areas and suggest interventions to improve safety. For example, AI could be used to analyze video footage from traffic cameras to detect dangerous driving behaviors and inform law enforcement or traffic management decisions.

10.6.4 Policy and Regulatory Changes

The successful implementation of AI and ML in Zambia's road network will require supportive policy and regulatory frameworks. These should address issues such as data privacy and security, algorithmic bias, and accountability for AI decisions. Zambia will need to balance the need to harness the benefits of AI/ML with the need to protect individual rights and societal values.

10.6.5 Partnerships and Capacity Building

Partnerships with universities, technical training programs, international tech companies, and development organizations can play a crucial role in building local capacity in AI/ML. These partnerships can help to develop the technical skills needed to implement AI/ML technologies and foster a culture of innovation in Zambia's transportation sector.

By harnessing the power of AI and ML, Zambia has the opportunity to leapfrog traditional stages of infrastructure development and usher in a new era of smart, sustainable, and efficient transportation. This could significantly boost the country's economic growth and development, positioning Zambia as a leader in transportation innovation in the region.

10.7 Navigating the African Digital Single Market: A Gateway to Progress for Zambia

As we explore the transformative potential of Artificial Intelligence (AI) and Machine Learning (ML) in Zambia's road network and transportation systems, it's crucial to consider the broader digital landscape of the African continent. One of the most significant milestones in this context is the progression towards an African Digital Single Market. This African Union-led initiative, backed by various global partners, aims to establish a unified digital marketplace across the continent, facilitating the unrestricted flow of goods, services, and data.

10.7.1 Opportunities for Zambia

For Zambia, a landlocked country often grappling with geographical constraints, the Digital Single Market presents a plethora of opportunities. It offers a platform for Zambian businesses to effortlessly reach consumers across Africa, overcoming traditional barriers to market access.

Moreover, the Digital Single Market could catalyze the integration of AI/ML technologies into Zambia's infrastructure strategy. With a unified digital space, data can traverse borders more freely, enabling more efficient data collection, analysis, and application. This could significantly boost the effectiveness of AI/ML in areas like infrastructure management, logistics, and supply chain optimization.

10.7.2 Investing in Digital Infrastructure and Skills

To fully harness the benefits of the Digital Single Market, Zambia must prioritize investments in digital infrastructure and skills development. This encompasses not only physical infrastructure, such as broadband networks, but also the 'soft' infrastructure of digital literacy and skills. Equipping Zambians with the necessary skills to navigate the digital world is crucial to ensure widespread benefits from the Digital Single Market.

10.7.3 Data Privacy and Security

As Zambia navigates towards the Digital Single Market, considerations around data privacy and security become paramount. The increase in data flows also escalates the risks associated with data breaches and misuse. Therefore, robust data protection measures must be established to safeguard the integrity of the digital space.

10.7.4 Conclusion: Embracing the Digital Future

In conclusion, the transition towards an African Digital Single Market presents significant opportunities for Zambia. By embracing this initiative and investing in the necessary digital infrastructure and skills, Zambia can position itself at the forefront of Africa's digital transformation. Harnessing the power of digital technologies, including AI and ML, can significantly enhance Zambia's road network, driving economic growth and propelling the nation towards a digitally empowered future.

10.8 Charting the Course: Integrating AI/ML into Zambia's Infrastructure Blueprint

As Zambia envisions its future, the integration of Artificial Intelligence (AI) and Machine Learning (ML) technologies into the country's infrastructure strategy becomes an imperative. The potential advantages of these technologies are immense, spanning from enhanced infrastructure management to optimized logistics and supply chains, and more data-driven decision-making processes that can catalyze economic growth.

10.8.1 AI/ML: Tools, Not Panaceas

However, it's essential to underscore that AI/ML technologies are not a cure-all. They are powerful tools that, when synergized with other strategies such as robust infrastructure investment, policy reforms, and capacity building, can yield optimal results. The deployment of AI/ML technologies should be part of a broader, comprehensive approach to infrastructure development that considers a range of factors and leverages a diverse array of tools and strategies.

10.8.2 Ethical Considerations and Equity

The implementation of AI/ML technologies must be undertaken with a keen eye on privacy, ethical, and equity issues. Given the data-dependent nature of these technologies, it's paramount to ensure data privacy is safeguarded and that the algorithms employed are transparent and free from bias. Moreover, the benefits derived from AI/ML should be equitably distributed, ensuring that all societal segments can reap the improvements these technologies can usher in.

10.8.3 Inclusivity: A Key Pillar

Inclusivity should also be a cornerstone of Zambia's AI/ML strategy. As AI/ML technologies become increasingly pervasive, there's a risk of creating a digital divide where those lacking the necessary skills or resources could be left behind. Therefore, measures to promote digital literacy and ensure that all Zambians have the opportunity to benefit from these technologies should be integral to Zambia's AI/ML strategy.

10.8.4 Conclusion: Embracing the Future

In conclusion, while the journey to implementing AI/ML technologies may be strewn with challenges, the potential rewards are substantial. By embracing these technologies and weaving them into its infrastructure strategy, Zambia can lay the groundwork for a more connected, efficient, and prosperous future. The journey may be intricate, but with careful planning, strategic investment, and a commitment to inclusivity and equity, Zambia can harness the power of AI/ML to revolutionize its road network and propel economic growth.

Reflection and Action Plan:

As we bring this book to a close, I encourage you to look more into the world of Artificial Intelligence (AI) and Machine Learning (ML), and their potential applications in infrastructure development.

Reflection Point:

Reflect on the question: How might AI and ML transform road infrastructure development in your country? Consider the various ways these technologies are already being used around the world, from predictive maintenance and traffic management to design and construction. How might these applications be adapted to your country's specific needs and challenges?

Action Plan:

Start by researching more about AI and ML, and their current and potential applications in infrastructure development. You might want to look into case studies of how these technologies have been used in other countries, or even reach out to experts in the field for their insights. Consider how these technologies could be integrated into your country's infrastructure development plans. Could they help to improve efficiency, reduce costs, or address specific challenges? Remember, the goal is to envision a future where technology and infrastructure development go hand in hand, driving progress and prosperity for your country.

As we conclude, remember that these action plans and reflection points are designed to engage you, the reader, and encourage you to think more deeply about the topics discussed in each chapter. Let's continue the dialogue and work together to make our vision a reality.

11

CONCLUSION

"Roads are the arteries through which the economy pulses. By linking producers to markets, workers to jobs, students to school, and the sick to hospitals, roads are vital to any development agenda." - Dr. Jim Yong Kim, former President of the World Bank.

As we conclude our journey through "Highways to Prosperity: The Economic Case for Road Infrastructure Development in Zambia," we have uncovered the transformative potential of road infrastructure in catalyzing economic growth and fostering societal development. A well-structured, robust, and efficiently maintained road network is not merely a conduit for transportation; it is a lifeline for trade, a beacon for investment, a generator of employment, and a catalyst for elevating living standards. It is, in essence, a bedrock of economic prosperity.

For Zambia, a landlocked nation nestled strategically in the heart of Southern Africa, the potential rewards of investing in road infrastructure are immense. By enhancing its road network, Zambia can not only stimulate its own economic growth but also etch out a role as a regional transportation hub, fostering economic integration and collaboration across Southern Africa. However, unlocking this potential is not an overnight task. It demands strategic planning, sustainable financing, robust governance, and a balanced approach to development that harmoniously aligns with other national priorities.

Moreover, the journey towards a prosperous future is not a solitary endeavor. It requires a collective effort, a harmonious symphony of collaboration involving policymakers, stakeholders, and the general public. As we embark on this path towards a brighter future, we must remember that the road to prosperity is not always a straight line. It is a path filled with twists and turns, bumps and potholes. But with unwavering determination, strategic foresight, and a shared vision, we can navigate these challenges and continue to forge ahead.

In the end, the journey is as important as the destination. For every kilometer of road we construct, we are not merely laying down asphalt or concrete. We are building bridges of connection, creating avenues of opportunity, and paving the path towards a brighter, more prosperous future. So, let's embark on this journey, Zambia. The highway to prosperity is within our reach.

Thank you for joining me on this enlightening journey. It is my hope that this exploration has offered valuable insights and sparked a meaningful conversation about the pivotal role of road infrastructure in Zambia's economic development. Let's keep this dialogue alive and work in unison to transform our shared vision into a tangible reality.

12

APPENDIX

I n this appendix, we look into the technical aspects and provide additional resources that can further enhance the reader's understanding of the topics discussed in the book. This section is designed to provide a more comprehensive understanding of the economic, social, and technological dimensions of road infrastructure development.

A.1 Economic Analysis

In this section, we explore more into the economic theories and models that underpin the arguments made in the book. We provide a more granular analysis of how road infrastructure impacts GDP, trade, and regional integration, drawing on economic theories and empirical evidence.

A.1.1 Economic Impact of Road Infrastructure on GDP

Here, we discuss the concept of the multiplier effect, which explains how investment in infrastructure can lead to an increase in economic activity that is several times the size of the initial investment. We also explore the concept of economic externalities, both positive and negative, that arise from road infrastructure development. This includes the indirect benefits that roads provide by enabling economic activities, as well as the potential costs associated with environmental degradation or social displacement.

The relationship between road infrastructure and Gross Domestic Product (GDP) is multifaceted and complex. Here, we review the economic theories and empirical evidence that underpin this relationship.

- **Multiplier Effect**

The multiplier effect is a key economic theory that explains how an initial investment can lead to an increase in economic activity that is several times the size of the initial investment. In the context of road infrastructure, the multiplier effect can be seen in the way that investment in roads can stimulate other sectors of the economy. For example, the construction of a new road can create jobs and stimulate demand in sectors such as construction, manufacturing, and retail. Over time, these effects can ripple through the economy, leading to an overall increase in GDP that is larger than the initial investment.

- **Economic Externalities**

Road infrastructure development also creates economic externalities, which are indirect benefits or costs that affect individuals or sectors of the economy that are not directly involved in the road project. Positive externalities of road infrastructure include improved access to markets, increased trade, and enhanced mobility. For example, a new road can make it easier for farmers to transport their produce to market, leading to increased agricultural sales and income. On the other hand, negative externalities could include environmental degradation or social displacement caused by road construction. These costs should be factored into the economic analysis of road projects.

- **Role of AI and ML**

Artificial Intelligence (AI) and Machine Learning (ML) can play a significant role in analyzing the economic impact of road infrastructure on GDP. For instance, ML algorithms can analyze historical data on road infrastructure investment and economic growth to predict the potential impact of future investments. This can provide valuable insights for policymakers and planners, helping them to make informed decisions about where to allocate resources.

In conclusion, the economic impact of road infrastructure on GDP is significant and mul-tifaceted. By understanding these dynamics, policymakers and planners can make informed decisions that maximize the economic benefits of road infrastructure development.

A.1.2 Road Infrastructure and Trade

This section provides a more detailed discussion of how improved road infrastructure can facilitate trade. We delve into the concepts of trade costs and trade facilitation, discussing how better roads can reduce the time and cost of transporting goods, thereby making trade more efficient and competitive. We also discuss how improved road connectivity can enhance access to markets, both domestically and internationally.

Road infrastructure plays a pivotal role in facilitating trade, both domestically and inter-nationally. In this section, we unravel the mechanisms through which road infrastructure impacts trade and the role of AI and ML in enhancing these impacts.

- **Transportation Costs**

One of the primary ways that road infrastructure impacts trade is through its effect on transportation costs. Good quality roads can reduce the time and cost of transporting goods, making it cheaper and easier for businesses to trade. This can lead to an increase in trade volumes, boosting economic activity and GDP. Conversely, poor quality roads can increase transportation costs, acting as a barrier to trade.

- **Market Access**

Road infrastructure also impacts trade by affecting market access. Roads connect producers with consumers, allowing goods to be sold in markets that would otherwise be inaccessible. This can particularly benefit rural areas, where farmers and other producers can use roads to access urban markets.

- **Role of AI and ML**

AI and ML can play a significant role in optimizing trade routes and predicting future trade flows. For example, AI algorithms can analyze traffic data and other variables to identify the most efficient routes for transporting goods. ML models can use historical trade data to predict future trade flows, helping businesses and policymakers to plan ahead and make informed decisions.

In conclusion, road infrastructure plays a crucial role in facilitating trade, with significant implications for economic growth and development. By leveraging AI and ML technologies, it's possible to further enhance these impacts, making road infrastructure an even more powerful tool for trade facilitation.

A.1.3 Road Infrastructure and Regional Integration

Here, we explore in further detail the role of road infrastructure in promoting regional integration. We discuss the theories of economic geography and regional economic integration, explaining how improved road connectivity can foster economic cooperation among neighboring countries, leading to increased trade, investment, and economic growth.

Road infrastructure is a key enabler of regional integration, fostering economic cooperation among neighboring countries. In this section, we explore the mechanisms through which road infrastructure impacts regional integration and the role of AI and ML in enhancing these impacts.

- **Facilitating Movement of Goods and People**

Roads are the physical links that connect different regions, facilitating the movement of goods and people across borders. By reducing travel times and transportation costs, good quality roads can make it easier for businesses to trade with neighboring countries, fostering economic integration.

- **Promoting Economic Cooperation**

By connecting different regions, road infrastructure can also promote economic cooperation. This can lead to increased investment, as businesses are able to access new markets and opportunities. It can also foster cultural exchange and understanding, further strengthening regional ties.

- **Role of AI and ML**

AI and ML can play a significant role in enhancing regional integration. For example, AI algorithms can be used to optimize cross-border logistics, reducing transportation costs and making it easier for businesses to trade across borders. ML models can also be used to predict future trade flows, helping policymakers to plan for and manage regional economic integration.

In conclusion, road infrastructure plays a crucial role in promoting regional integration, with significant implications for economic growth and development. By leveraging AI and ML technologies, it's possible to further enhance these impacts, making road infrastructure an even more powerful tool for regional integration.

A.1.4 The Role of Artificial Intelligence and Machine Learning in Economic Analysis

Artificial Intelligence (AI) and Machine Learning (ML) are powerful tools that can revolutionize the way we analyze economic data and make predictions. In this section, we look at how these technologies can be applied to the economic analysis of road infrastructure.

- **Predictive Analysis**

Machine Learning algorithms can analyze historical data on road infrastructure investment and economic growth to predict the potential impact of future investments. These predictions can help policymakers make informed decisions about where to allocate resources for maximum economic impact. For example, ML models could predict which road projects are likely to have the greatest impact on GDP growth or job creation, helping to prioritize investments.

- **Trade Flow Analysis**

AI can also be used to analyze large datasets on trade flows and transport costs. By analyzing patterns in these data, AI algorithms can provide valuable insights for policymakers and planners. For example, AI could identify key trade corridors where improved road infrastructure could have the greatest impact on reducing transport costs and boosting trade.

- **Economic Forecasting**

AI and ML can also be used for economic forecasting, helping to predict future trends in economic growth, trade, and other key indicators. These forecasts can provide valuable information for long-term planning and strategy development.

In conclusion, AI and ML offer powerful tools for economic analysis, providing insights that can help to optimize road infrastructure investments. By leveraging these technologies, policymakers and planners can make more informed decisions, maximizing the economic impact of road infrastructure development. This detailed economic analysis is intended to provide readers with a deeper understanding of the economic concepts discussed in the book and to demonstrate the potential of AI and ML in economic analysis.

A.1.5 Economic Impact of Road Infrastructure on Job Creation

Road infrastructure development is a significant source of job creation, both directly and indirectly. In this section, we delve deeper into the mechanisms through which road infrastructure impacts job creation and the role of AI and ML in enhancing these impacts.

- **Direct Job Creation**

The construction and maintenance of roads require a significant amount of labor, leading to direct job creation. These jobs can range from low-skilled labor positions to high-skilled engineering and management roles.

- **Indirect Job Creation**

Beyond the direct jobs created by road construction and maintenance, road infrastructure can also lead to indirect job creation. By improving connectivity and reducing transportation costs, roads can stimulate economic activity, leading to job creation in a variety of sectors. For example, better roads can make it easier for farmers to access markets, leading to growth in the agricultural sector and associated job creation.

- **Role of AI and ML**

AI and ML can play a significant role in enhancing job creation associated with road infrastructure. For example, AI can be used to optimize construction processes, reducing costs and making it feasible to undertake more road construction projects, leading to more job creation. ML can be used to predict where road improvements will have the greatest economic impact, helping to prioritize investments in a way that maximizes job creation.

In conclusion, road infrastructure plays a crucial role in job creation, with significant implications for economic growth and development. By leveraging AI and ML technologies, it's possible to further enhance these impacts, making road infrastructure an even more powerful tool for job creation.

A.2 Technical Specifications of Road Infrastructure

In this section, we delve into the more technical aspects of road infrastructure development, providing a deeper understanding of the engineering considerations, standards for road construction, and advanced methods for road maintenance and repair.

A.2.1 Engineering Considerations

Engineering considerations form the backbone of any road infrastructure project. They encompass a broad spectrum of factors that determine the feasibility, durability, and safety of the road network. Here, we get into some of these key considerations:

- **Geotechnical Investigations**

Before any road construction project begins, a thorough geotechnical investigation is necessary. This involves studying the soil and rock conditions of the proposed construction site. The findings from these investigations are crucial in determining the type of foundation required for the road, the potential for landslides or soil erosion, and the need for any soil stabilization measures. The geotechnical investigation can also influence the choice of construction materials and techniques.

- **Drainage Design**

Another critical aspect of road construction is the design of the drainage system. Proper drainage is essential to prevent waterlogging and subsequent damage to the road surface and substructure. This involves designing features such as ditches, culverts, and stormwater drains to effectively channel water away from the road. The drainage design must consider local rainfall patterns, topography, and soil permeability.

- **Pavement Design**

The design of the pavement, or the road's surface layer, is a complex process that depends on several factors. These include the expected traffic loads, the local climate, and the materials available for construction. The pavement must be designed to withstand the wear and tear of traffic and weather conditions while providing a smooth and safe driving surface. This involves choosing the right materials (such as asphalt, concrete, or gravel), determining the appropriate thickness of the pavement layers, and considering the need for features like skid resistance and reflectivity.

- **Safety Measures**

Road design must also incorporate safety measures to protect motorists, pedestrians, and cyclists. This can include features like guardrails, pedestrian crossings, bike lanes, and traffic signs. The design should also consider visibility, especially at intersections and curves.

In conclusion, engineering considerations are a vital part of road infrastructure development. They ensure that the road network is safe, durable, and fit for purpose. By understanding these considerations, we can appreciate the complexity of road construction and the expertise required to build a robust and efficient road network.

A.2.2 Standards for Road Construction

Road construction standards are a set of guidelines and specifications that ensure the safety, durability, and functionality of a road network. These standards, often developed by national or international bodies, cover a wide range of aspects, from the design phase to the materials used in construction. Here, we delve into some of these key standards:

- **Road Width**

The width of a road is a crucial factor that determines its capacity and safety. Standards for road width vary depending on the type of road (e.g., highway, arterial road, residential street) and the expected volume of traffic. For instance, highways designed for high-speed, high-volume traffic typically require wider lanes and shoulders to accommodate vehicles safely. On the other hand, residential streets with lower traffic volumes may have narrower lanes. These standards ensure that roads are designed to handle their intended traffic safely and efficiently.

- **Pavement Thickness**

The thickness of the pavement is another critical standard in road construction. This is determined based on the expected traffic loads and the strength of the underlying soil. A road expected to carry heavy trucks, for example, will need a thicker pavement than a residential street with light traffic. The pavement thickness is crucial for the road's durability and lifespan, as it helps to distribute the weight of vehicles and prevent damage to the underlying layers of the road.

- **Surface Material**

The choice of surface material is also governed by road construction standards. This can range from asphalt and concrete for high-traffic roads to gravel or earth for low-traffic rural roads. The choice of material depends on several factors, including the expected traffic, local climate, and available resources. For instance, asphalt is often preferred for its durability and smoothness, but it requires significant resources to produce and maintain. On the other hand, gravel or earth roads are cheaper to construct but may require more frequent maintenance.

In addition to these, road construction standards also cover other aspects such as drainage design, signage and markings, safety features, and environmental considerations. Adhering to these standards is essential to ensure that roads are safe, durable, and fit for their intended use. By understanding these standards, we can appreciate the complexity of road construction and the importance of careful planning and design in building a robust road network.

A.2.3 Advanced Methods for Road Maintenance and Repair

Maintaining and repairing roads is a critical aspect of infrastructure management. It ensures the longevity of the road network, enhances safety, and optimizes the economic benefits derived from the infrastructure. Here, we delve into some advanced methods used in road maintenance and repair:

- **Surface Treatments**

Surface treatments are used to restore the road's surface, improve skid resistance, and seal small cracks. These treatments, such as chip seals or micro-surfacing, involve applying a thin layer of asphalt and aggregate to the road surface. This not only improves the road's appearance and ride quality but also extends its lifespan by protecting the underlying layers from water damage and wear.

- **Pavement Recycling**

Pavement recycling is an innovative method of road repair that involves reusing the existing pavement material. This can be done in place (on the road) or in a plant (off-site). The process involves removing the old pavement, crushing it, and mixing it with new material to produce a high-quality road surface. This method is not only cost-effective, as it reduces the need for new materials, but also environmentally friendly, as it reduces waste and energy use.

A.2.4 Intelligent Transportation Systems (ITS)

ITS use technology to improve road safety and efficiency. For example, traffic sensors can provide real-time data for traffic management, helping to optimize traffic flow and reduce congestion. Digital signs can provide drivers with timely information about road conditions, traffic, and incidents, enhancing safety and efficiency. In addition, predictive analytics, powered by AI and ML, can be used to predict maintenance needs, allowing for proactive road management.

These advanced methods represent the cutting edge of road maintenance and repair. They highlight the potential of technology and innovation in enhancing the efficiency and effectiveness of road infrastructure management. By understanding these methods, we can appreciate the complexity of road maintenance and the importance of continuous innovation in delivering high-quality, sustainable road infrastructure.

A.3 Additional Data

In this section, we delve into a more detailed examination of the data and statistics that underpin Zambia's road network and its economic impact. This includes a comprehensive look at road density, road quality, transportation costs, and the contribution of the transportation sector to Zambia's GDP.

A.3.1 Road Density and Quality

Road density refers to the total length of the country's road network relative to its land area. It is a critical indicator of the accessibility and connectivity of different regions within the country. In Zambia, road density is relatively low, reflecting the country's vast land area and the challenges of providing road infrastructure in sparsely populated rural areas. However, there are significant disparities in road density and quality between urban and rural areas, with urban areas generally having a higher road density and better-quality roads.

A.3.2 Transportation Costs

Transportation costs are a significant factor in the overall cost of doing business and can impact the competitiveness of a country's goods and services in the global market. In Zambia, transportation costs are relatively high due to factors such as long distances, poor road conditions, and inefficiencies in logistics and supply chains. These high costs can act as a barrier to trade and investment, underscoring the need for improvements in road infrastructure and logistics.

A.3.3 Contribution of the Transportation Sector to GDP

The transportation sector, which includes road, rail, air, and water transport, plays a crucial role in Zambia's economy. According to the World Bank, Zambia's economy rebounded in 2021, with real GDP growing at 4.6%, supported by firmer copper prices, favorable external demand, good rainfall, and post-election market confidence. The transportation sector contributes significantly to this growth, facilitating the movement of goods and people, connecting markets, and providing employment. However, the sector's potential is not fully realized due to challenges such as inadequate infrastructure and high transportation costs.

A.3.4 The Role of AI and ML in Economic Analysis

Artificial Intelligence (AI) and Machine Learning (ML) technologies have the potential to revolutionize economic analysis by providing more accurate and timely data, enabling more precise forecasting, and facilitating more informed decision-making. For example, ML algorithms can analyze historical data on road infrastructure investment and economic growth to predict the potential impact of future investments. AI can also be used to analyze large datasets on trade flows and transport costs, providing valuable insights for policymakers and planners.

These additional data and statistics provide a more detailed picture of the current state of Zambia's road network and its economic impact. They underscore the importance of investing in road infrastructure to boost economic growth, improve competitiveness, and enhance the quality of life for the Zambian people.

A.4 Impact of Road Infrastructure on Economic Indicators

Several studies have shown a positive correlation between road infrastructure and various economic indicators, such as GDP growth, trade volumes, and investment levels. These studies provide empirical evidence of the potential economic benefits of improving Zambia's road network.

- A study by Calderón and Servén (2004) titled **"The Effects of Infrastructure Development on Growth and Income Distribution"** Found that there is a significant positive correlation between infrastructure development, including road infrastructure, and economic growth. The study also found that infrastructure development contributes to income distribution and reduces income inequality.

- A report by the World Bank titled **"Road Infrastructure and Economic Development: Some Diagnostic Indicators"** found that road infrastructure development has a significant impact on economic development. The report found that countries with better road infrastructure have higher economic growth rates and better economic performance.

- A study by Banerjee, Duflo, and Qian (2012) titled **"On the Road: Access to Transportation Infrastructure and Economic Growth in China"** found that road infrastructure development has a significant positive impact on economic growth in China. The study found that counties in China that were connected to the national highway system experienced higher economic growth rates than those that were not.

These studies provide empirical evidence of the potential economic benefits of improving Zambia's road network. They underscore the importance of road infrastructure development in promoting economic growth, facilitating trade, and attracting investment. They also highlight the potential role of AI and ML in enhancing the efficiency and effectiveness of road infrastructure development.

A.5 Case Study References

For readers interested in further exploring the case studies mentioned in the book, this section provides detailed references and links to the original sources.

China's Belt and Road Initiative (BRI) "The Belt and Road Initiative: Progress, Contributions and Prospects." Office of the Leading Group for the Belt and Road Initiative.

India's Golden Quadrilateral Highway Network Ghosh, I., & De, P. (2004). "The Golden Quadrilateral Project: Assessing the Success and Identifying the Challenges." Economic and Political Weekly, 39(31), 3465-3471.

Brazil's Infrastructure Investment Pereira, A. M., & Andraz, J. M. (2013). "On the economic effects of public infrastructure investment: A survey of the international evidence." Journal of Economic Development, 38(4), 1-37.

United States Highway Network System Duranton, G., & Turner, M. A. (2012). "Urban growth and transportation." The Review of Economic Studies, 79(4), 1407-1440.

German Autobahn Baum-Snow, N. (2007). "Did highways cause suburbanization?" The Quarterly Journal of Economics, 122(2), 775-805.

Trans-African Highway Network "Trans African Highways." United Nations Economic Commission for Africa.

AI and ML in Road Infrastructure (Singapore) "AI in Traffic Management." Land Transport Authority, Singapore.

These references provide a starting point for readers interested in delving deeper into the case studies discussed in the book. They offer a wealth of information and insights on the role of road infrastructure in economic development and the potential of AI and ML in transforming road networks.

A.6 Recommended Readings - Books and Texts

For readers interested in further exploring the topics discussed in this book, the following resources provide valuable insights into the economics of infrastructure, the history of road development, and the future of transportation:

"The Road Taken: The History and Future of America's Infrastructure" by Henry Petroski

This book provides a comprehensive history of America's infrastructure and offers insights into the challenges and opportunities that lie ahead.

"The Economics of Transport: A Theoretical and Applied Perspective" by Jonathan Cowie

This book offers a detailed exploration of transport economics, with a focus on policy implications.

"Infrastructure: A Guide to the Industrial Landscape" by Brian Hayes

This book provides a fascinating tour of the physical infrastructure that makes modern life possible.

"The Big Roads: The Untold Story of the Engineers, Visionaries, and Trailblazers Who Created the American Superhighways" by Earl Swift

This book tells the story of the people who designed and built the U.S. highway system.

"Transportation Infrastructure Engineering: A Multimodal Integration" by Lester A. Hoel, Nicholas J. Garber, and Adel W. Sadek

This textbook provides a comprehensive introduction to transportation engineering, with a focus on integrating different modes of transportation.

"Artificial Intelligence in Transportation: Information for Application" by National Academies of Sciences, Engineering, and Medicine

This report provides an overview of the potential applications of AI in transportation and offers recommendations for transportation agencies.

"The Belt and Road Initiative: What Will China Offer the World in Its Rise" by Wang Yiwei

This book provides an in-depth analysis of China's Belt and Road Initiative and its implications for global development.

These resources offer a wealth of information and insights that can complement and deepen the understanding gained from this book. They are highly recommended for anyone interested in the economics of infrastructure, the history and future of road development, and the transformative potential of AI and ML in transportation.

A.7 Recommended Articles and Reports

For readers interested in delving deeper into the topics discussed in this book, the following articles and reports provide valuable insights into the relationship between road infrastructure and economic development:

"Road Infrastructure and Economic Development: Some Diagnostic Indicators" by Aschauer, David Alan (World Bank, 1990)

This report provides an analysis of the relationship between road infrastructure and economic development, offering diagnostic indicators to assess the impact of road infrastructure on economic performance.

"Transport Infrastructure and Economic Growth" by Banister, David and Berechman, Joseph (Journal of Transportation and Statistics, 2001)

This article explores the complex relationship between transport infrastructure and economic growth, providing a comprehensive review of empirical studies on the topic.

"The Role of Infrastructure in Development: Insights from Recent Literature" by Estache, Antonio (The International Bank for Reconstruction and Development / The World Bank, 2010)

This report provides a review of recent literature on the role of infrastructure in development, offering insights into the impact of infrastructure on economic growth, income distribution, and poverty reduction.

"Infrastructure and Economic Growth in Asia" by Bhattacharyay, Biswa Nath (Asian Development Bank Institute, 2013)

This report provides an analysis of the impact of infrastructure on economic growth in Asia, offering valuable insights for other developing regions.

"The Belt and Road Initiative and the SDGs: Towards Equitable, Sustainable, Resilient Development Goals" (United Nations Development Programme, 2018)

This report explores the potential of the Belt and Road Initiative to contribute to the achievement of the Sustainable Development Goals, including through infrastructure development.

"Artificial Intelligence - The Revolution Hasn't Happened Yet" by Michael Jordan (Harvard Business Review, 2018)

This article provides a balanced perspective on the potential and limitations of AI, offering valuable insights for policymakers and practitioners considering the application of AI in various sectors, including transportation.

These resources offer a wealth of information and insights that can complement and deepen the understanding gained from this book. They are highly recommended for anyone interested in the economics of infrastructure, the history and future of road development, and the transformative potential of AI and ML in transportation.

A.7 Glossary of Terms

This section provides definitions for key terms and concepts used throughout the book. Understanding these terms will enhance your comprehension of the discussions and arguments presented.

Road Infrastructure: Refers to the physical network of roads, including associated structures such as bridges, tunnels, and traffic management systems.

Gross Domestic Product (GDP): The total monetary or market value of all the finished goods and services produced within a country's borders in a specific time period. It serves as a comprehensive measure of a nation's overall economic activity.

Public-Private Partnership (PPP): A cooperative arrangement between one or more public entities and one or more private entities. In the context of infrastructure, PPPs often involve a private entity financing, constructing, and managing a project, with the public entity providing guarantees or support.

Regional Integration: The process by which individual states within a geographic region, increase their level of interaction and cooperation, often through the creation of regional organizations spanning several nations.

Road Density: A measure of the total length of a country's roads relative to its total land area. It is often used as an indicator of a country's infrastructure development.

Pavement: The durable surface material laid down on an area intended to sustain vehicular or foot traffic, such as a road or walkway.

Geotechnical Investigation: An examination of the physical properties of soil and rock around a site to design earthworks and foundations for proposed structures and for repair of distress to earthworks and structures caused by subsurface conditions.

Intelligent Transportation Systems (ITS): The application of advanced information and communication technologies to transport infrastructure and vehicles in order to improve their safety, reliability, and efficiency.

Road Fund: A dedicated fund for road maintenance, often financed by user charges such as fuel levies or tolls. It is typically used to ensure a steady source of funding for road maintenance and upgrades.

Green Bonds: A type of bond that is specifically earmarked to raise money for climate and environmental projects. These bonds are typically asset-linked and backed by the issuer's balance sheet, and are also tax-exempt.

Artificial Intelligence (AI): The simulation of human intelligence processes by machines, especially computer systems. These processes include learning (the acquisition of information and rules for using the information), reasoning (using rules to reach approximate or definite conclusions) and self-correction.

Machine Learning (ML): A type of artificial intelligence that allows software applications to become more accurate in predicting outcomes without being explicitly programmed. The basic premise of machine learning is to build algorithms that can receive input data and use statistical analysis to predict an output value.

Supply Chain: A network between a company and its suppliers to produce and distribute a specific product or service to the final customer. This network includes different activities, people, entities, information, and resources.

Predictive Maintenance: Techniques designed to help determine the condition of in-service equipment in order to predict when maintenance should be performed. This approach promises cost savings over routine or time-based preventive maintenance.

Traffic Management: The planning, monitoring and control of traffic from one place to another to ensure a safe, smooth and efficient transport system.

Autonomous Vehicles: Also known as self-driving cars, these vehicles combine sensors and software to control, navigate, and drive the vehicle.

Digital Single Market: A strategy by the European Union to ensure access to online activities for individuals and businesses under conditions of fair competition, consumer and data protection, removing geo-blocking and copyright issues.

Data Infrastructure: An organization's entire collection of hardware, software, networks, data centers, facilities and related equipment used to develop, test, operate, monitor, manage and/or support information technology services.

Regulatory Framework: A model people can use for reforming and creating regulations, especially in major sectors and companies affecting the public.

Capacity Building: The process by which individuals and organizations obtain, improve, and retain the skills, knowledge, tools, equipment, and other resources needed to do their jobs competently.

Digital Literacy: The ability to use information and communication technologies to find, evaluate, create, and communicate information, requiring both cognitive and technical skills.

Algorithmic Bias: Systematic and repeatable errors in a computer system that create unfair outcomes, such as privileging one arbitrary group of users over others.

Digital Transformation: The integration of digital technology into all areas of a business, fundamentally changing how you operate and deliver value to customers. It's also a cultural change that requires organizations to continually challenge the status quo, experiment, and get comfortable with failure.

Big Data: Extremely large data sets that may be analyzed computically to reveal patterns, trends, and associations, especially relating to human behavior and interactions.

Data Mining: The process of discovering patterns in large data sets involving methods at the intersection of machine learning, statistics, and database systems.

Data Privacy: The aspect of information technology that deals with the ability an organization or individual has

to determine what data in a computer system can be shared
with third parties.

Data Security: Protective digital privacy measures that
are applied to prevent unauthorized access to computers,
databases and websites.

Data Analysis: A process of inspecting, cleansing, transforming, and modeling data with the goal of discovering
useful information, informing conclusions, and supporting
decision-making.

These definitions should provide a helpful reference for readers as they navigate the technical
language of road infrastructure economics and development.

A.5 References

This section provides a comprehensive list of all the sources and references cited throughout the book. These references offer readers the opportunity to explore more the topics discussed and explore the original sources of information.

Aschauer, David Alan. "**Road Infrastructure and Economic Development: Some Diagnostic Indicators.**" World Bank, 1990.

Banister, David and Berechman, Joseph. "**Transport Infrastructure and Economic Growth.**" Journal of Transportation and Statistics, 2001.

Estache, Antonio. "**The Role of Infrastructure in Development: Insights from Recent Literature.**" The International Bank for Reconstruction and Development / The World Bank, 2010.

Petroski, Henry. "**The Road Taken: The History and Future of America's Infrastructure.**" Bloomsbury Publishing, 2016.

Cowie, Jonathan. "**The Economics of Transport: A Theoretical and Applied Perspective.**" Routledge, 2009.

Hayes, Brian. "**Infrastructure: A Guide to the Industrial Landscape.**" W. W. Norton & Company, 2014.

World Bank. "**Transport Overview.**" www.worldbank.org

International Transport Forum. www.itf-oecd.org

Road Development Agency Zambia. www.rda.org.zm

U.S. Department of Commerce. (2022). "**Zambia: Distribution and Sales Channels.**" Retrieved

from `https://www.trade.gov/country-commercial-guides/zam`
`bia-distribution-and-sales-channels`

These references serve as a valuable resource for readers who wish to further their understanding of the economic implications of road infrastructure development, particularly in
the context of Zambia.

In memory of my brother Griffin, who in his trials, taught me that life's challenges can be our greatest teachers. His journey continues to inspire my work.

About the Author

Mabvuto V. Kaela is an innovative thinker, proficient data analyst, and a fervent believer in the transformative potential of infrastructure development. His unique perspective, shaped by a non-linear career path and a deep understanding of economic concepts, has led him to coin the term "Ideaonomist" to describe his role. Born and nurtured in Zambia, Mabvuto relocated to the United States to pursue advanced education. He embarked on his academic journey studying Finance and Economics at the University of Pittsburgh, later earning his Bachelor's degree from the California University of Pennsylvania. His quest for knowledge led him to acquire a Master's degree in Data Analytics from Robert Morris University. Mabvuto's professional trajectory spans across diverse industries, where he has applied his economic acumen and data analytics expertise in various roles. These experiences have endowed him with a comprehensive perspective on economic development and a profound comprehension of the pivotal role data and analytics play in steering strategic decisions.In recent times, Mabvuto has cultivated a profound interest in the realm of Artificial Intelligence (AI) and Machine Learning (ML). He perceives these technologies as powerful catalysts for economic growth and societal advancement, especially in developing nations like Zambia. To share his insights and passion, he founded the AI4Africa Progress newsletter on LinkedIn, which explores the transformative impact of AI/ML on developing nations. In his book, "Highways to Prosperity: The Economic Case for Road Infrastructure Development in Zambia", Mabvuto amalgamates his unique ideas, data analytics capabilities, and passion for development to present a persuasive argument for investing in road infrastructure. His aspiration is for this book to not only enlighten and motivate its readers but also ignite a dialogue about how Zambia and similar developing nations can capitalize on infrastructure development to construct a prosperous future. This book offers a thorough yet comprehensible examination of the significance of road infrastructure for Zambia's economic development. It stands as a rallying cry for policymakers and the general populace, underscoring the potential advantages of investing in road infrastructure and providing a strategic blueprint for achieving this goal.